WHEN HE COMES

Michelle Maddox

WHEN HE COMES

Published by About Face Books

ISBN: 979-8-9943873-2-0

First Edition

Book Design by Sabryna Washington

TABLE OF CONTENTS

An Introduction To Love.

WHEN HE COMES, IT WILL BE WITH HIS LOVE. A LOVE WE HAVE NEVER EXPERIENCED.

THEN OUR LORD PRAYED, ***"YOUR WILL BE DONE ON EARTH AS IT IS IN HEAVEN"***, HE KNEW EXACTLY WHAT THE FATHER'S WILL WAS, AND IS, AND EXACTLY HOW IT WOULD COME ON EARTH AND TO EARTH.

As you read WHEN HE COMES the follow up book to *'THE BLIND DATE, THE MISSING LINK TO BRIDAL READINESS'*, you will also know exactly what the Father's will is and exactly how it will come.

It is no longer a mystery. We have spent all of time since the garden of Eden in our frail human efforts to bring His will to Earth but now He is releasing the mysteries of His eternal will and how it will come to the Earth. It is actively coming, even as we speak, into the Earth. And it is nothing that we have ever seen or heard before. IT IS A MOVE NO ONE IS YET AWARE OF. It has never taken place before in the truth and the completeness of how His will is indeed actively and currently coming to Earth.

He has shared not only the truth of what He is doing. He is actively doing what is shared in these books.

As vessels chosen to be those who walk in full redemption of the Mind of Christ, we are not walking around with our head in the sand. We are walking around with our head in HIS MIND, THE MIND OF CHRIST!

WE WELCOME YOU HERE TO THESE PAGES. WE INVITE YOU TO ENTER HIS HEART AND TO REMAIN IN HIS HEART WITH US AS YOU READ THE REALITY, NOT THE INFORMATION, OF HIS WILL ON EARTH AS IT IS IN HEAVEN.

NOTES

Chapter 1
WHAT WAS THAT?

'WHEN HE COMES' moves us from knowing Him as the cornerstone, to carrying Him as His vessel of the capstone.

Welcome to *'WHEN HE COMES'*, a book regarding the soon coming of Christ the King of Redemption. Leading into this first chapter of this new book I want to make reference to the prior book Christ the King wanted released. The title of that book is, *'THE BLIND DATE, THE MISSING LINK TO BRIDAL READINESS.'*

Making reference to that prior book is not to sell that book or this book. The writing of these two books is strictly due to the Lord showing me to do so. In that book as well as this one, I am establishing that I am not a writer or an experienced author. I am His obedient vessel, and this is something He has clearly directed me to do. These books are not properly edited, they are self published, and they are strictly for the readiness of the Bride for HIS SOON return. Furthermore, these books are written with a very repetitive style. The Lord has referred to this repetition of content as climbing Mount Zion. Step after step after step. He has a purpose for the writings within these books containing much repetition as the reader progresses. **THE TRUTHS WITHIN THESE BOOKS HAVE BEEN PERFECTED BY HIS VOICE AND HIS LIFE, BUT THE ACTUAL WRITING, COMPILATION, AND PRESENTATION OF THE BOOKS ARE NOT PERFECTED. THEY ARE SIMPLY AVAILABLE FOR YOU TO GRASP HIS TRUTH AND LET IT DWELL IN YOUR INTERNAL.**

DO NOT QUIT BECAUSE OF REPETITIONS. PUSH FORWARD. AS STATED, HE HAS A DIVINE PURPOSE FOR THE DYNAMIC OF THE REPETITIONS. FOR HE IS CHISELING AWAY AT THE FALLEN AND CURSED MIND OF MAN ALL OF MANKIND INHERITED IN THE GARDEN FROM THE CHOICES OF ADAM AND EVE.

I highly recommend you read, *'THE BLIND DATE... THE MISSING LINK TO BRIDAL READINESS'* prior to, along with, or following this book titled, *'WHEN HE COMES'*.

Simply put, *'THE BLIND DATE, THE MISSING LINK TO BRIDAL READINESS'*, comes down to two powerful truths:

1. ***THE BLIND DATE* is where we get to know the vastness of Christ we have never known.** The vastness of Christ, the King of Redemption. The vastness that goes far beyond what we have known so far and continues throughout all of eternity with the unfolding of who He really is.

2. ***THE MISSING LINK* is allowing Christ Himself to annihilate Jesus of Nazareth to the point Jesus no longer exist, so we can become intimate with Christ the King existing from the foundations of the Earth before the need for Jesus due to the fall of mankind.** Allowing HIM to annihilate HIS PAST identity OF JESUS, so we can embrace the FULL IDENTITY of the vastness of the original intention creation of Christ the King, hence *'THE BLIND DATE'*.

These truths go hand-in-hand and heart-to-heart with Christ the King regarding what He is indeed currently already doing, and what is indeed soon to be fulfilled.

In the prior book titled *'THE BLIND DATE'*, we have already established the "new breed" of His Apostles and Prophets are the Manchild of Revelation 12. They are His READY vessels. They are the mature and ready Bride redeemed unto HIS original intention from the foundations of the Earth. It is not our job to figure this out. Our position is to let Christ the King annihilate all logical thinking, opinions, and judgments as to who these people should be, what they should look and sound like, and how they should operate. He is absolutely defying ALL logic within how He is doing this. **As long as we process through the logical, fallen, and CURSED mind we inherited from the fall of mankind in the garden with Adam and Eve, we will miss this beautiful and so very sovereign move HE is currently and actively making.**

I will insert here at the beginning, something already shared and explained in *'THE BLIND DATE'* in order to establish where we are coming from and where we are continuing within this book. On February 4 of 2022, He came to my bedside and made an announcement. He simply spoke, ***"I am about to make THE MOVE NO ONE IS YET AWARE OF."***

Over a course of time He opened His heart and shared 'the move no one is yet aware of' is HIS move back to the foundations of the Earth, where His original intention over mankind, the Earth, and each individual was created. His original intention before the fall of mankind when Adam and Eve ate the deception of doubt. He shared His heart of how it was and is a highly sovereign move. Sovereign, meaning we cannot initiate it or stop it. Sovereign meaning only HE can initiate it, and only HE can choose who participates based on our faith, belief, and readiness. Since then, we have become very aware. We are no longer totally blind regarding the move He is indeed already making that He announced He was going to make. There is already a small group of people not only being intellectually made aware, but experientially in the internal made aware of His move back to His original intention over all of mankind. His original intention before the fall which brought in death, disease, financial lack, toil, sweat of the brow, hardships, etc.

REDEEMING US BACK TO HIS ORIGINAL INTENTION WHERE HE TRULY FULLY ABIDES AND DWELLS IN HIS PEOPLE, HIS VESSELS. REMOVING EVERYTHING ASSOCIATED WITH THE FALL INCLUDING AGING, DISEASE, DEATH, AND DYING, BUT NOT LIMITED TO THOSE ASPECTS. REDEEMING US BACK TO HIS ORIGINAL INTENTION OF FULL DOMINION AND AUTHORITY OVER EVERY AREA OF OUR LIVES AND THE EARTH. REDEEMING US BACK TO TRUE VESSELS OF CHRIST THE KING.

REDEEMING US INTO VESSELS OF WHO HE REALLY WAS, IS, AND FOREVERMORE WILL BE. TAKING US AND PLANTING US INTO THE TRUTH OVER HIS EXISTENCE, WHILE ANNIHILATING THE LIMITATIONS AND EVEN THE DECEPTIONS OF WHO WE BELIEVE HIM TO BE.

'THE BLIND DATE' lays the beautiful foundation of how He is replacing the fallen and cursed mind of man with the redeemed Mind of Christ, how He is defying all logic, how He is annihilating the identity of the Bride, as well as the identity of Jesus, unto CHRIST THE KING OF REDEMPTION, along side with sharing details of this very beautiful and sovereign move He is currently making.

This book is going to take us beyond the solid and firm truth and foundations of not only what He is currently doing, but how He is currently doing it, and why He is doing it unto the dynamics of the very near future of WHEN HE COMES. *'THE BLIND DATE'* is the foundation for the beautiful truth on the following pages of *'WHEN HE COMES.'*

Let's go ahead now and establish the truth of *'WHEN HE COMES'* not being what the traditional church teaches. **The Second Coming of Christ established well within His written word is when He completely fills HIS READY BRIDE with HIS LIGHT of Isaiah 60, HIS LIFE, LIGHT, AND LOVE of the entire book of John, along with the Sevenfold Sprits of God, to return to the Earth and rule and reign within His vessels.** To rule and reign with Him includes operating in the full government of Heaven, loving with a love we have never experienced before, and setting the captives free. We are all captive to a fallen mind. Religion is captivity, deception is captivity, mental disorders, mental illnesses, sicknesses, and disease, are all forms of captivity. As well as strongholds, addictions, and everything not existing in redemption, all being forms of captivity.

The purpose of *'WHEN HE COMES'* is not to rewrite *'THE BLIND DATE'*, but to take us from those well established truths into what He has revealed thus far of what life will be like, ON EARTH WITHIN HIS VESSELS once the sovereign move He is making is complete and we find ourselves no longer waiting. **This move He is currently making and which is no longer on hold, will fill and send HIS BRIDE back, fully changed, completely filled, and equipped to rule and reign with HIM!**

"I am the Alpha and the Omega", says the Lord God," the one who WAS, and who IS, and who IS TO COME, the Almighty."

'WHEN HE COMES' takes us beyond the beautiful and sovereign truth of *'THE BLIND DATE, THE MISSING LINK TO BRIDAL READINESS'*, and into being His fully redeemed vessels SENT BACK TO THE EARTH TO RULE AND REIGN WITH HIM! TO RULE AND REIGN WITH CHRIST THE KING OF REDEMPTION.

'WHEN HE COMES' moves us from knowing Him as the cornerstone, to carrying Him as His vessel of the capstone.

'WHEN HE COMES' takes us into the vastness of His Second Coming within His chosen vessels and takes us deeper and deeper for all of eternity.

HE IS TO BE GLORIFIED IN THE EARTH and this glorification takes place within and through His chosen and redeemed vessels who will carry His LOVE, LIGHT, AND LIFE to a lost and dying world.

'THE BLIND DATE' challenged us to go beyond courting Him and into actually marrying Him as His ready and chosen vessels. The redeemed of the Lord of Psalm 107 who have the "say so" (the FULL AUTHORITY) of Christ the King. The Bride equally yoked with Him AS HE IS, ruling and reigning with HIM!

One's question might be, "well since HE is doing it, and it is the move HE is indeed making, why do I need to know all of this contained within '*THE BLIND DATE*' as well as '*WHEN HE COMES*"?

My answer to anyone wondering the same is that HE is indeed doing it. It is indeed HIS SOVEREIGN MOVE. It is indeed all by HIS HAND. However, He does it in our lives in the internal abiding place of Christ in response to our surrender to Him. The most beautiful surrender we can give Him is to believe this is indeed what He is currently, actively, and quickly doing. The most beautiful surrender we can give Him is to believe it with all our heart. As we believe and we surrender everything we thought we knew, and as we surrender everything we knew Him to be, He does it!

This is a sovereign move. It is also a challenging move. It challenges everything we have been taught and told. Everything we thought and reasoned and figured out. It is the mystery of the hidden treasures within His written word which are all unlimited expressions of Him.

THE TRUTH THAT HE IS NOT CAPTURING US INTO A RAPTURE TO KEEP US WITH HIM AND PROTECT US FROM WHAT WE CALL "END TIMES AND HARD TIMES" AND HELL ON EARTH, BUT YET RETURNING US TO EARTH FILLED WITH HIS LIGHT, LIFE AND LOVE TO CARRY HIS GLORIFIED, PERFECTED, AND COMPLETE REDEMPTION, IS AN UNLIMITED EXPRESSION OF HIM.

HE IS CALLING HIS READY VESSELS TO HIM, TO FILL THEM AND SEND THEM BACK!

💣 IT'S ALL HIM!

💣 IT'S ALL UNLIMITED EXPRESSIONS OF HIM!

- IT'S HIS LIFE.
- IT'S THE INTERNAL POSSESSION OF THE MENORAH, WHICH STANDS BEFORE THE THRONE.
- IT'S HIS LIFE ETERNAL.
- IT'S THE SEVENFOLD SPIRITS OF GOD.
- IT'S HIS FIRE.
- IT'S HIS LIGHT.
- IT'S HIS DNA. THE DNA OF HIS BLOOD!
- IT'S HIS LOVE AND THE LOVE OF THE FATHER WE HAVE NEVER EXPERIENCED!
- IT'S HIS MOLECULAR STRUCTURE TAKING OVER OUR FALLEN PHYSICAL BODIES AND BRINGING US BACK TO HIS ORIGINAL INTENTION CREATION IN THE FOUNDATIONS OF THE EARTH!
- IT'S HIS VOICE.
- IT'S THE MANIFESTED SONS OF ROMANS 8.
- IT'S THE MAN CHILD OF REVELATION 12.
- IT'S THE REDEEMED OF THE LORD OF PSALM 107.
- IT'S THOSE WHO RETURN FROM THE WOMB OF THE DAWN DRESSED IN HIS DNA OF PSALM 110.
- IS THE FIVE WISE VIRGINS WITH OIL IN THEIR LAMPS READY FOR CHRIST!

- IT'S THE HOT VESSELS, NOT THE WARM OR THE COLD VESSELS of REVELATIONS 3:15-16!
- IT'S THE SAVIORS, DELIVERERS, AND JUDGES OF OBADIAH 21.
- IT'S THOSE WHO DO GREAT EXPLOITS OF DANIEL 11.
- IT'S THE BRIDE OF CHRIST OF THE BOOK OF REVELATION.
- IT'S THE AUTHORITY OF THE 144,000 OF REVELATION 11.
- IT'S THE READY BRIDE OF REVELATION 19.
- IT'S THE VOICE OF THE SPOKEN WORD OF ZACHARIAH 4 THAT CAUSES A MOUNTAIN TO LITERALLY BECOME A PLAIN!
- IT'S ALL EXPRESSIONS OF HIM!
- IT'S ALL VESSELS OF HIS FULLNESS!
- IT'S ALL VESSELS EQUIPPED AT HIS THRONE AND SENT BACK TO THE EARTH WITH FULL UNLIMITED EXPRESSIONS OF HIS LIFE AND HIS LIFE!

'THE BLIND DATE, THE MISSING LINK TO BRIDAL READINESS' paves the road to 'WHEN HE COMES'.

These books challenge and confront religion, traditions of men, doctrine, and even man made prophecies never of Him. These books even challenge things **HE HIMSELF INDEED ONCE SAID OF WHICH HE IS NO LONGER FULFILLING BECAUSE HIS EYES HAVE SEARCHED TO AND FRO, AND HE HAS FOUND THOSE COMPLETELY SURRENDERED UNTO HIM OF WHOM HE CAN FILL AND SEND BACK FOR............WHEN HE COMES!**

He is coming in the internal of HIS vessels my dear friends and THAT IS THE SECOND COMING OF CHRIST!

HOW DID WE EVER MAKE HIM REMAINING IN THE ETERNALS AND REMOVING HIS PEOPLE TO HIMSELF BE ANYTHING ABOUT HIM COMING? WHEN THAT FALSE THEORY IS ALL ABOUT US LEAVING AND HIM STAYING AWAY FROM IT ALL?

HOW DID HIM STAYING AND CALLING US UP TO HIM EVER GET TRANSLATED INTO HIM RETURNING OR COMING, WHEN THAT IS HIM STAYING?

'*WHEN HE COMES*' IS ABOUT THE TRUTH OF WHEN HE ACTUALLY COMES,... not about Him staying and calling us to stay with Him. THE SECOND COMING OF CHRIST, FULLY POSSESSING THE INTERNAL OF HIS CHOSEN VESSELS!

Christ truly COMING!!!

WHICH IS EXACTLY WHY WE ARE TOLD TO BE A BRIDE MADE READY. NOT A BRIDE READY TO LEAVE AND STAY GONE. BUT A BRIDE READY TO BE FILLED AND COME BACK WITH HIM INTERNALLY POSSESSING HER TO RULE AND REIGN, FOR THIS IS TRULY......

WHEN HE COMES!

NOTES

Chapter 2
LOOK UP!

"Look Up For Your Redemption
Draws Nigh!"

Anyone reading this type book is already well aware of His letters in red where He directs us to ***"Look up for our redemption is nigh."*** Our redemption is indeed drawing near. Some translations use the word deliverance in place of redemption. For redemption is indeed deliverance from captivity. And the specific captivity He is delivering us from, redeeming us from, is the captivity of the curse of the fallen mind of man when the fall of mankind took place in the garden with Adam and Eve. For the fallen mind of man is indeed a curse in direct opposition to His original intention of creation.

The scriptures proceeding Luke 14:28 speak of times of distress and perplexity in the nations as to when we are to look for our redemption to draw nigh. In comparison to Revelation 19, which tells us His return is in response to a Bride making herself ready. Point being, there is a parallel of time where there is indeed perplexity in the nations lining up with the readiness of His mature Bride. And that my dear friends is where we are.

He comes in RESPONSE to a ready Bride, but His return COINCIDES with the nations being in an uproar.

We are in the time to LOOK UP!

We miss it when we think as His Bride, our only responsibility is to look upward into the sky to watch for Him. This redemption begins with our responsibility to look INWARD and see if we are indeed ready. As we walk out the readiness process with Him, we are to look up first and INTO THE MIND OF CHRIST. For redemption comes when the Mind of Christ completely overtakes the fallen mind of Man. As we LOOK UP, into the mind of Christ, everything changes. Everything rearranges. We gain what I like to refer to as HEAVEN'S PERSPECTIVE.

HEAVEN'S PERSPECTIVE IS WHEN THE STRATEGY OF HEAVEN, WHICH IS DIVINE ORDER, BEGINS TO BECOME WAY MORE REAL FOR US THAN THE PHYSICAL WORLD IN WHICH WE LIVE!

We need to establish right here it is the spiritual realm which is real. The physical realm is not. However, as fallen humans with fallen minds from the fall of mankind, we focus on the physical. We focus on the land we walk upon, the house we live within, the floors on which we stand, the ceilings which cover us, the furniture on which we sit and lie, the clothes we wear, the food we eat, everything we see, and feel with touch, and smell, and taste, and hear.....and we must know the physical is all deception!

This is because the physical is fallen and cursed from the fall of mankind.

➲ The spiritual is real...The spiritual is real...The spiritual is real.

➲ THE SPIRITUAL IS TRUTH!...THE SPIRITUAL IS TRUTH!

As we "look up" to THE MIND OF CHRIST, we are looking into the spiritual. We are looking into what is real! WE ARE LOOKING INTO TRUTH! We are looking into REDEMPTION!

As He has indeed been speaking in the internal of those who are actively on the road to redemption, no longer only knowing He is about to make the move no one is yet aware of, but becoming more and more aware of the move He is making by actively looking up into the Mind of Christ, He has been directing us to go higher! Taking us higher into the Mind of Christ.

Coming up higher, is ultimately to go higher than the physical world in which we live. Higher than what we call natural. After all, we are three part beings, which are two part spiritual, and only one part physical. We are spirit, we are soul, and we are physical body. Our bodies are the physical houses of spiritual beings. And the spiritual is what is real! One part physical body encompasses our two part spiritual existence of soul and spirit. Yet so many people who are indeed one part physical, and two part spiritual, will say they do not believe in the spiritual. And this is a perfect example of how deceived, distracted, and misled we are by the physical. The physical lies to us as being real because it's what we see. While all along the spiritual is real, and carries the weight of everything!

The Mind of Christ is like a best seller cookbook. Full of recipes, formulas, measurements, and specific outcomes. The Mind of Christ is superior to high-level mathematics. Solving problems, dilemmas, equations, and giving formulas for perfected outcomes. The Mind of Christ supersedes the fallen mind so much. We cannot relate at all unless we first believe the spiritual is real and the physical is false deception. Even our human bodies which contain the Life of Christ are deceptive forms of the human body He formed for us in the foundations of the Earth with His original intention for us before the fall of mankind.

Redemption not only restores the Mind of Christ and kicks out the cursed and fallen mind of man, it restores the physical body of original intention created for us in the foundations of the Earth before the fall produced our fallen minds and fallen physical bodies.

For those of us who have been on this walk with Him for a little over four years now of going higher into the Mind of Christ to look up for our redemption, which is getting very close, we are already experiencing others witnessing Christ dwelling within us. Others are commenting on physical beauty. They are commenting on seeing a love come forth from our eyes. They are commenting on seeing the internal light of Christ from ***Isaiah 60... "Arise and shine for your light has come."***

PEOPLE WE KNOW ARE COMMENTING, AND TOTAL STRANGERS ARE STARING, AND TAKING A SECOND LOOK WHILE COMMENTING ON SEEING BEAUTY, LIGHT, AND LOVE!

THIS IS PROOF COMING FORTH INTO THE EXTERNAL OF THE RESIDING OF CHRIST THE KING IN THE INTERNAL OF THESE VESSELS!

How can this be? How can it be there are people/vessels already possessing a level of redemption so real and so full even without saying a word about it, onlookers are seeing the internal light, love, and fire?

It starts with focusing on and believing the spiritual. It starts with leaving the natural and fallenness behind and coming up higher with Him to reside in the residence of spiritual truth. To reside in the Mind of Christ!

Coming up higher is to leave fallenness behind and live from redemption rather than from our fallen state. Choosing higher! Making decisions higher! Thinking higher! Coming up higher is a different mindset. We set our minds on the Mind of Christ and we live, breathe, and operate from the higher level of His invitation to COME UP HIGHER!

HIGHER is not a place of stagnation. Higher is a place of movement within His Life which keeps going higher and continues to go higher and higher IN HIM and WITH HIM to the full culmination and the full manifestation of redemption IN HIM!

THIS BOOK IS WRITTEN FROM A POSITION OF HIGHER as well as the prior book of *'THE BLIND DATE, THE MISSING LINK TO*

BRIDAL READINESS'.

It is important we lean into, step into and learn to reside in the Mind of Christ in order to embrace the powerful truth within both books. The spiritual is way more real. Because it is the real! There is actually no comparison between the reality of the spiritual realm versus the physical realm which is fallen and cursed. Not just our minds fallen and our bodies fallen, but the entire fallen realm we live in pales, greatly pales in comparison to the reality of the spiritual realm. The spiritual realm is real and it's where spiritual events take place. They don't take place in this fallen realm we are so familiar with. We have exhausted ourselves by operating within the fallen realm of thinking and the fallen realm in which we live to see the manifestation of the Second Coming of Christ. The Second Coming of Christ will only and currently is only taking place in the spiritual realm of coming up higher!

We are to labor for Christ in the spiritual rather than the natural for all laboring in the natural is vain and empty laboring.

Adam related to the things of the Earth while also being able to walk with God without limitation, but God's purpose for Adam was beyond the Earthly and into spiritual dominion. Adam fell from God's plan for him because of the fall of mankind. HE FELL FROM GOD'S ORIGINAL INTENTION OF PERFECTION AND INTO A LIFE OF DECEPTION. We, those of us called to be His ready Bride, are not only called beyond the fallen and into Spiritual Dominion, HE has placed us there with HIM with HIS invitation to come up higher. **The process we have been in since He announced, *"I am about to make the move no one is yet aware of"*.....The process which He is actively making and has made us more and more aware of.....is the internal work of Christ that takes us from the seed of salvation unto the full manifestation of vessels of Christ.**

He alerted us to it. We said yes, Lord! But HE is the one who does the internal work. He gives us the knowing of what He is doing, and we cooperate with it.

BUT IT IS HE WHO DOES IT IN US!

He has shown us that our souls/our minds, our existence has been placed by His hand into spiritual dominion, which is the higher ground!

THE HIGHER GROUND OF THE MIND OF CHRIST!
WE ARE TO REMAIN THERE STEADFAST!

The word of God defines steadfast as being firm, determined and unwavering in one's belief and position in Christ with emphasis being on, IN CHRIST.

Not simply learning about Christ, knowing about Christ, following Christ or walking with Christ. But being internally IN Christ and Christ internally IN us.

AS ONE!

FURTHERMORE, HE IS NOT COMING FOR A HAREM OF BRIDES. HE IS COMING FOR ONE CORPORATE BRIDE WHO HAS GROWN INTO ONE WITH HIM AND ONE WITH EACH OTHER. WHERE THERE IS NO DIVISION OF CHRIST AND HIS ENTIRE CORPORATE BRIDE BETWEEN HIM AND HER AND HER AND EACH OTHER. A ONENESS. AN EXISTENCE OF ONE. AN EXISTENCE OF ONE CONSISTING OF CHRIST PLUS HIS ENTIRE CORPORATE BRIDE, WHICH EQUALS ....ONE.

ONE CHRIST, PLUS ONE CORPORATE BRIDE, EQUALS... ONE!

Nothing within the above truth is stating we have any ability to go higher and remain steadfast in the higher ground.

It all comes by Him and His ability. IT ALL COMES BY HIS SOVEREIGN MOVE. And that is where we often slip. We think that if we have any active fallenness in our minds, if we are thinking something we don't know or understand... Anything from the fallen mind of mankind... We think if we are aware of any fallenness, that we have failed the higher ground. What He wants us to know from the Mind of Christ, not information but Life from the Mind of Christ is that...

HE called us to the higher ground. HE put us there. And HE is maintaining our position in the higher ground. Therefore, when we are aware of fallenness, we are to be more aware of the higher ground. Which is HIM. Which has always been HIM. Which is the Mind of Christ. And we are to immediately shift into the steadfastness that is possible and has been given to us by HIS hand. The steadfastness of remaining in the higher ground of the Mind of Christ. Of HIM.

We must know from the Mind of Christ, the position of the higher ground and retaining the position of the higher ground, along with the steadfastness of the higher ground, IS ALL DONE BY HIS HAND!

THE REQUIREMENT ON US IS TO BELIEVE THIS. WE MUST BELIEVE WHAT HE IS DOING AND WILLINGLY PARTICIPATE WITH WHAT ONLY HE AND HE ALONE CAN DO AND IS DOING AND WILL REMAIN TO DO. HE IS THE HIGHER GROUND. HE IS THE ONE WHO INVITED US THERE. HE IS THE ONE WHO KEEPS US THERE.

IT IS THE HIGHER GROUND OF REDEMPTION UNTO HIS ORIGINAL INTENTION BEFORE THE FALL OF MANKIND!

AND IT ALL COMES FROM THE SPIRITUAL REALM!

WE MUST WILLINGLY SHIFT AND ALLOW HIM TO SHIFT OUR

FALLEN AND CURSED MIND OF MAN INTO THE MIND OF CHRIST AND PLANT US THERE. STEADFAST IN HIM, AND WITH HIM.

Within the Mind of Christ He has shown and is continuing to show, as well as actively do and tangibly make us more and more aware of what He is doing. Day by day we ARE aware of the move He is indeed currently making that no one was once aware of. We are becoming more and more aware each day, as we willingly stay connected to the spiritual realm and acknowledge His hand of movement to go higher and remain higher in the Mind of Christ.

It is within the higher ground of the Mind of Christ where molecular structure changes take place!

The molecular structure of our fallen souls change into the molecular structure of the soul created in His original intention of the likeness of the Father, the Son, and the Holy Spirit. It is the molecular structure of 'MADE IN OUR IMAGE', that changes from a fallen molecular structure into the molecular structure of the image of the divine Trinity.

As the molecular structure of our souls change.....As the molecular structure advances into His divine perfection of His original intention, it begins to affect the molecular structure of our physical bodies. Youth is restored, health is restored, aging is reversed, death is redeemed. We must really get a grip on this! We must really get a grip on how we have limited Him and HIS VASTNESS and HIS LOVE for us and what He has intended for us all along!

He wants us to know going back-and-forth from fallenness to the knowing of the Mind of Christ is not our failure at this point in the process. For how can it be our failure when He is the one making this sovereign move? Otherwise, if it were failure, it would be His failure.

This does not mean we have no part or participation. WE MUST STAY ENGAGED WITH WHAT HE IS DOING! This does not mean we wallow around in fallenness and make fallen choices. Or camp out in the fallen mind, or dwell on the fallen situations or thoughts or even fallen things we must overcome in Him.

IT MEANS HE IS AWARE AND WANTS US EQUALLY AWARE THAT HE IS THE STEADFASTNESS OF THE HIGHER GROUND OF MOLECULAR STRUCTURE!

FOR ULTIMATELY TO LOOK UP, WHICH IS TO GO HIGHER IN HIM, IS TO GO HIGHER INTO THE IDENTITY AND THE MOLECULAR STRUCTURE OF THE IMAGE OF THE FATHER, THE SON, AND THE HOLY SPIRIT. TO BECOME VESSELS OF HIS KINGDOM AND NOT SIMPLY VESSELS OF HIS SEED!

We are in the active and tangible transition of our fallen nature into full redemption of HIS original intention. We are in the transition, but moreso we are living in the reality that we can remain in the higher ground without any episodes of fallenness by grabbing tight to Him as the steadfastness of redemption.

He is showing us that within the higher ground we are able, because of Him, to immediately and swiftly transition from any fallen deception, confusion, or negativity back into the higher ground of the Mind of Christ for that is now our new residence!

HE WANTS US ALREADY, EVEN NOW, LIVING FROM THE REDEEMED MIND OF CHRIST AND NOT JUST ACCESSING IT WHEN NEEDED. IT IS TO BE OUR NEW ADDRESS OF RESIDENCE!

He wants us accessing the higher redeemed Mind of Christ and living from the sure knowings of the Mind of Christ rather than the filthy logic of the fallen mind. He wants us to corporately go higher and be in one accord of living, thinking, processing, discussing, and moving forward on a much higher level. For the higher ground of the Mind of Christ encompasses everything we need now and forevermore.

- THE HIGHER GROUND OF THE MIND OF CHRIST IS HIS MOLECULAR STRUCTURE!
- IT IS HIS LIGHT THAT COMES INTO THE WORLD TO JUDGE THE WORLD!
- IT IS HIS LOVE THAT WILL DO MORE THAN WE EVER THOUGHT HIS POWER WOULD DO!
- IT IS THE LOVE OF THE FATHER LIVING INSIDE US THROUGH WHICH WE WILL BE ABLE TO LOVE OTHERS RATHER THAN THE FALLEN LOVE WHICH EVEN AT ITS BEST DAY PALES IN COMPARISON TO THE LOVE OF GOD!
- IT IS HIS KINGDOM!
- IT IS HIS SEVENFOLD SPIRITS OF GOD!
- IT IS THE GREAT I AM!
- FOR HE IS THE BLINDING LIGHT, HE IS THE BURNING BUSH, HE IS THE ROD OF MOSES!
- WHEN WE EMBRACE, LIVE AND BREATHE THROUGH THE TRUTH AND REALITY OF THE SPIRITUAL REALM, LEAVING THE CURSED AND FALLEN REALM BEHIND US, WE LIVE IN ONENESS WITH THE GREAT I AM!
- AND THIS, MY DEAR FRIENDS IS HOW WE RULE AND REIGN WITH HIM. THIS IS HOW WE TURN OUR NATION

AROUND!

- 💣 THIS IS HOW WE DO IT!
- 💣 WE DO IT BY BELIEVING!
- 💣 WE DO IT BY LOOKING UP!
- 💣 WE DO IT BY RISING UP!
- 💣 AND WE DO IT BY REMAINING IN HIM, WITH HIM IN US GROWING FROM THE SEED OF SALVATION INTO THE FULL MANIFESTED LIFE OF CHRIST, THE KING OF REDEMPTION!

When we go higher and remain higher, we are not shaken! Remaining in higher ground means to no longer try to figure anything out. Figuring things out involves the cursed and logical fallen mind. In the higher ground of the Mind of Christ, the knowings are available and clear. The knowings are concrete and solid. The peace is tangible. As the process of living through the higher ground of the Mind of Christ continues and develops, we leave all religion behind for religion is formed with cursed, logical, and analytical thinking completely void of the freedom of the LIFE of Christ, which is the MIND of Christ.

Recently, I was speaking His Life over someone and the Lord spoke in my internal... ***"LOCK, STOCK, AND BARREL!"***

I looked up the phrase to find out what it really meant, and it means to be 100%, to be complete, without anything overlooked or left out!

THE HIGHER GROUND WHICH OF COURSE IS A DEEPER AND HIGHER LEVEL OF THE MIND OF CHRIST, IS THE HIGHER GROUND OF LOCK, STOCK, AND BARREL! 100% complete, nothing overlooked or left out!

When we look up for our redemption and live from the Mind of Christ rather than the mind of man, we are living with His stamp of approval. His certificate of guarantee. His peace that indeed passes all understanding of the fallen mind. We live in the sure knowings of the Mind of Christ, which come with complete freedom! We live from REDEMPTION!

This is important to remember... As we go higher in Him, the lies and deception of the physical world in which we still currently live, and from the fallen mind which is still currently active at least in some small degree, there will be appearances of delay. Any appearance of delay or failure is part of the lie and the deception of this fallen realm we continue to reside in for a short time remaining. The completion of all things in Him is in the higher realm where our internal is residing and He is taking us higher into.

WE WILL FOREVERMORE ONCE WE ENTER THE HIGHER GROUND, THE SPIRITUAL REALM OF THE MIND OF CHRIST, CONTINUE FOR ALWAYS AND FOREVER TO GO HIGHER AND HIGHER AND HIGHER INTO THE VASTNESS OF THE MIND OF CHRIST WE ARE TRULY ACTIVELY BEGINNING TO LIVE FROM, BUT HAVE ONLY TAPPED INTO EVEN AS FANTASTIC AS IT HAS BEEN THUS FAR!

Knowing to rise up. Knowing to look up into the higher ground of the Mind of Christ. Knowing to stay there. Knowing to be in one accord with Him and the corporate Bride in the position of the higher ground of the Mind of Christ. Along with the tangible, very aware space of experiencing the Life and Peace of the higher ground of the Mind of Christ, is evidence, evidence, evidence, evidence of a current and active change of the molecular structure of the fallen mind into the molecular structure of the original intended mind of glory from the foundations of the Earth!

AS WE GO HIGHER AND CONTINUE TO GO HIGHER IN HIM, MORE MOLECULAR STRUCTURE CHANGE TAKES PLACE! THE WATER OF THE SOUL IS ACTIVELY BEING CHANGED BY WAY OF MOLECULAR STRUCTURE INTO THE NEW WINE WHICH IS HIS FINEST DEMONSTRATION THAT WE HAVE FINALLY ARRIVED AT...

HIS TIME!

In John 2 of the account of the wedding and the water turned to wine, He stated... ***"It is not YET my time."***

THEN, PAY ATTENTION TO THESE WORDS,......
THEN, HE DEMONSTRATED HOW TO STEP INTO HIS TIME WHEN HE DID INDEED TURN THE WATER TO THE VERY BEST WINE, EVEN AFTER STATING IT WAS NOT YET HIS TIME!

WE ARE CURRENTLY TO FOLLOW THAT DEMONSTRATION AND STEP INTO THE TIME OF THE MIND OF CHRIST REPRESENTED BY THE WATER POTS.

WE ARE TO STEP INTO THE TIME OF THE CHANGE OF MOLECULAR STRUCTURE, REPRESENTED BY THE WATER TURNED INTO WINE AND LIVE FROM REDEMPTION, EVEN NOW!

EVEN WHILE IT IS NOT YET FULLY TIME FOR HIM TO CALL HIS CHOSEN VESSELS TO HIM AND SEND THEM BACK.

WE ARE TO FOLLOW HIS DEMONSTRATION AND STEP INTO AND OPERATE FROM THE TIME WE ARE STILL WAITING TO BE COMPLETELY FULFILLED!

Because dear Bridal friends, IT IS NOW HIS TIME!

- WE ARE CURRENTLY LIVING IN HIS TIME!
- THE TIME OF THE NEW WINE!
- FOR THE NEW WINE IS THE MIND OF CHRIST!
- THE NEW WINE OF THE MIND OF CHRIST IS THE NEW WINE OF THE VASTNESS OF CHRIST TO BE POURED OUT FOR ALL OF ETERNITY!
- THE NEW WINE OF THE MIND OF CHRIST IS HIS VASTNESS.
- IT IS A LOVE WE HAVE NEVER KNOWN.
- IT IS A PEACE WE HAVE NEVER KNOWN.
- IT IS TRUE ONENESS.
- IT IS HIS HEART FOR HIS CHURCH.
- IT IS HIS BRIDE.
- IT IS THE SEVENFOLD SPIRITS OF GOD.
- IT IS THE KINGDOM OF GOD.
- IT IS REDEMPTION.
- IT IS PERFECTION.
- IT IS HIS ORIGINAL INTENTION BEFORE THE NASTY FALL OVERTOOK US ALL!
- IT IS THE GOVERNMENT OF HEAVEN!
- AND IT IS NOW ......HIS TIME!

Look up! Your redemption is just around the corner! Look up! Go higher! Look up into the Mind of Christ and go higher in the Mind of Christ and continue to go, go, go, go higher and higher and higher into His Light, His Life, and His Love of the Mind of Christ that changes the dynamics of everything!

WE MUST RAISE OUR AWARENESS OF WHAT HE IS CURRENTLY DOING AND STAY THERE! WE MUST RAISE OUR AWARENESS THAT HE IS INDEED MAKING THE MOVE NO ONE WAS ONCE AWARE OF, BUT SOME ARE ACTIVELY BECOMING MORE AND MORE AWARE OF DAY BY DAY.
THE MOVE BACK TO HIS ORIGINAL INTENTION!

When He completes the move back to His original intention, it will be completed at His throne. His ready Bride who are residing in the Mind of Christ will be called up. They are the ones who will be raptured out.

BUT!! .....PLOT TWIST.........They will be sent BACK!

They will be sent back as the Manchild of Revelation 12. Those with the complete authority of Christ to rule and reign the nations with the rod of iron which is HIMSELF residing in the internal of HIS ready and mature Bride!! A Bride without spot or wrinkle. A Bride without deceptions and religion. A Bride without the spots and wrinkles of the fallen soul that brings deceptions, rules, regulations, religion and analytical thinking. Spots and wrinkles are not personal sins and failures!

Spots and wrinkles come from the deception and damage of the fallen mind of man that have produced deceptions, religion, rules, regulations.

SPOTS AND WRINKLES ARE THE DECEPTIONS AND LIMITATIONS THE FALLEN AND CURSED MIND OF MAN HAS

PLACED ON AND WITHIN US REGARDING THE TRUE CHRIST OF REDEMPTION!

The mature Bride desperate for His return WITHIN HER to rule and reign with Himself, the rod of iron, is without a fallen mind therefore, without spots and wrinkles.

SHE IS WITHOUT SPOTS AND WRINKLES BECAUSE SHE IS WITHOUT THE FALLEN AND CURSED MIND OF MAN. SHE RESIDES WITHIN THE MIND OF CHRIST!

WE MUST RAISE OUR AWARENESS OF WHAT HE IS INDEED CURRENTLY DOING. WE MUST RAISE THAT AWARENESS TO A VERY HIGH LEVEL AND STAY THERE!

John 3:19 tells us that "His light comes into the world to judge the world". The book of John also tells us the light came to expose the darkness and expel the darkness, and the darkness did not and could not comprehend the light. The darkness could not overcome the light!

His Light has come exactly as John 3 says, to expose darkness in the Earth.

However, it is currently exposing the darkness and misconceptions and deceptions of the soul WITHIN HIS BRIDE, for it is the weight of deception within the soul that is holding the soul back from redemption into the Mind of Glory.

As the soul is cleansed by His likeness and His light, His light comes to expose the darkness of the nations. We also know Isaiah 60 says,***'deep darkness will cover the whole Earth and the peoples, and the glory of the Lord will rise upon you!'*** His Light and glory of Isaiah 60 is already beginning to shine as the result of those already not only looking up, but... LIVING UP!

THOSE LOOKING UP AND LIVING UP IN THE CURRENT AND ACTIVE REDEMPTION, WHICH WILL SOON BE COMPLETE!

WHEN THIS REDEMPTION IS COMPLETE IN THOSE WHO HAVE BEEN WILLING TO LOOK UP, GO UP, AND LIVE UP, THAT MY DEAR FRIENDS IS THE SECOND COMING OF CHRIST WITHIN THE INTERNAL OF HIS MATURE BRIDE TO BE SENT BACK TO RULE AND REIGN THIS NATION AND BRING IT FROM DEEP, DARK CORRUPTION INTO......

AMERICA, THE LAND OF THE REDEEMED!

THIS REDEMPTION WILL MOVE TO OTHER NATIONS OF THIS EARTH UNTIL THE EARTH AND THE FULLNESS OF IT ARE COMPLETELY HIS IN PERFECT REDEMPTION OF HIS ORIGINAL INTENTION!

For much and most of this process of HIM making the move, (back to His original intention before the fall of mankind), no one is yet aware of, He responded to our SURRENDER OF SELF. He now has our will. We have fully surrendered all self and self will to Him and in doing so, HE HAS TAKEN US HIGHER IN HIM.

He is now responding to our MINDSET. As we set our minds to His mind and go higher in our thinking, believing, thoughts, choices, decisions and every aspect of how we do life, He responds to that new mindset of us going higher to His mind, and HE TAKES US HIGHER IN HIM.

With our full surrender of self, and now our mindset connected to the Mind of Christ, we are becoming one with Him which qualifies us as a Bride made ready.

When I say us, I am not limiting that to those of us who have been on this walk and this higher journey the last four years. I'm talking about any of us reading and believing and

stepping into the higher truth of His return shared in *'THE BLIND DATE'* as well as *'WHEN HE COMES.'*

CONTINUE LORD, CONTINUE!

NOTES

NOTES

Chapter 3
ON YOUR MARK, GET SET, GO!

"The One calling you is faithful, Who will also do it."

There is an urgent need for complete readiness from His chosen elite Bride so He can come forth and fully make the move He is indeed making. Even though this is very true, the pinnacle and mountain peak of the readiness will take place as the man child of Revelation 12 is caught up to His throne. In His presence, we will be fully equipped as complete vessels of Christ the King of Redemption to come back and rule and reign with the full authority of the government of Heaven, consisting of the Sevenfold Spirits of God. However, there is a vital readiness prior to standing before Him. But in standing before Him, the entire authority of Heaven will be granted to His chosen. The chosen will return to a mighty army of mature Bride who were not included in this first elite group, and together His complete corporate Bride will shake things up. Move things, rearrange things, and speak with the breath of God to a mountain and it will indeed become a plain.

This chapter is being written as great encouragement for ALL His Bride! Much advancement of readiness and closeness of time has changed, even since writing *'THE BLIND DATE.'* The great encouragement within this chapter is how *'THE BLIND DATE'* referred to not much time left and how readiness was an emergency, an imperative emergency! We are now able to share advancement of time and readiness, even since *'THE BLIND DATE'* was released in January 2026. So much advancement of readiness as well as time, a book can now be written referring to... *'WHEN HE COMES'*, including proof of advancement of readiness and time even in a very few short months!

Until He calls us to Him to do the complete work of readiness before He calls us to Him to fully equip us with His DNA, which is His love, His government, His justice, the full Mind of Christ, until then, He is challenging us to go higher and live higher IN HIM! To live from a place IN HIM, not 'about' Him. A place WITHIN HIM that is higher than the fallen world we live. He is calling us and challenging us, He is inviting us, encouraging us and urging us to come up higher. To change our mindset. To set our mind on the Mind of Christ, which is vastly higher than our fallen minds and our fallen world and lives.

He is inviting and challenging us to begin operating on higher ground EVEN NOW.

WHY? BECAUSE HE HAS TAKEN US TO HIGHER GROUND IN HIM!

In order to participate with Him in HIS challenge to go higher, we must know more of who He is beyond Jesus of Nazareth. We must know Christ the King of Redemption. We must know what He means by His original intention from the foundations of the Earth. **We must know His challenge to go higher is the reality of Him bringing us into the vastness of Christ we have never known. Raising our thoughts, decisions, choices, outlook, our very positions to enter and live from the matrix of His original intention for us, our families, and our nation.**

We spoke much in '*THE BLIND DATE*' of staying in cadence with Him. AND NOW, His current cadence is a last lap, final curve cadence. We also spoke that the return of Christ, His true Second Coming, which is within the internal of His ready Bride, His ready vessels, is not a set time, but rather it is a culmination of time. This was to show us the readiness of His chosen continues and runs face-to-face into Him, producing the CULMINATION of time, producing the moment of "WHEN HE COMES" being the Second Coming of Christ. His return which looks and will be totally different than the limited place we have lived thus far.

For to even believe He is removing us is a great limitation on the vastness of who He is. Fallen minds for centuries have so limited the beauty of His vastness. The only outcome has been from the matrix of that which states we are removed. Yet the reality of the depth of His Life and the sheer vastness of who He truly is, is a much bigger and more beautiful reality than the fallen mind could even begin to comprehend.

MOST HAVE NEVER EVEN CONSIDERED OR GIVEN THE LEAST BIT CREDIT TO THE TRUTH OF WHAT HE'S REALLY DOING. THE TRUTH IS DEBUNKED BECAUSE HE IS SO INCREDIBLY VAST IT OFFENDS OUR FALLEN MINDS. OUR FALLEN AND CURSED MINDS HAVE BEEN SO OFFENDED BY HIS VASTNESS, WE HAVE COME UP WITH A MUCH LESSER PLAN OF LIMITATION. THE TRUTH IS, OUT OF THAT VASTNESS, HIS PLAN IS TO FULLY STEP INTO US AND SEND US BACK CARRYING THAT SAME VASTNESS TO RULE, REIGN, CONQUER, DIVIDE, SEPARATE, AND BRING VICTORY TO THE EARTH!

WE HAVE DUMBED HIM DOWN TO HIS ONLY OPTION BEING TO YANK US OUT AND TUCK US AWAY WHILE THE EARTH GOES TO HELL IN A HANDBASKET WHATEVER THE HECK A HANDBASKET IS!

HE IS NOT TO BE DUMBED DOWN BY THE FALLEN AND CURSED MIND. WE ARE TO LET HIM OFFEND OUR FALLEN AND CURSED MINDS OF HOW WE HAVE LIMITED THE ONE WE CALL SAVIOR AND LORD TO NOT BE ABLE TO DO IT ANY OTHER WAY THAN TO REMOVE US WHEN THE REALITY IS, HE IS IN THE PROCESS OF FILLING US!

HOW WE HAVE LIMITED HIM!

BUT PRAISE GOD ALMIGHTY, HE IS NOT LIMITING HIMSELF NOR HIS CHOSEN BRIDE DESPERATE ENOUGH TO BELIEVE THERE IS A VASTNESS THAT WILL TAKE ALL OF ETERNITY TO UNFOLD. THAT SAME VASTNESS IS ENTERING HIS CHOSEN EVEN NOW AND WILL INCREASE AND INCREASE AND INCREASE WHILE IT OFFENDS AND OFFENDS AND OFFENDS,

AND IN THE MEANTIME, SET THE CAPTIVES FREE!

Also, in *'THE BLIND DATE'* much was said of how our role is to surrender, and He responds to our surrender by coming internally and doing the work.

He does everything! But we must cooperate.

What I want to share now in this chapter, is that where we once surrendered, and He responded by moving deeper and deeper into the internal, we are now at a place IN HIM where He is responding to our mindset being on His mind of the vastness of who He is.

- **He once responded to our surrender.**
- **Now He is responding to our mindset.**

- **Our surrender was the process.**
- **Our mindset is the purpose.**

With that being said, not only has He changed what He is responding to from responding to surrender and now responding to mindset, that now changes redemption coming forth in a CULMINATION OF TIME WE ARE WALKING INTO, to now being A SET TIME WE ARE RESIDING INSIDE OF!!

Readiness had us heading into a CULMINATION of time.

Now readiness has brought us into the mindset of vastness. The mindset unto the Mind of Christ has produced a SET TIME we are RESIDING WITHIN FOR HE IS TIME!

A SET TIME of residing anticipation, rather than a CULMINATION OF TIME of deeper readiness.

This is why He is emphasizing mindset on the vastness of

Christ, where we live from redemption even now. It is because of a SET TIME, overriding a CULMINATION of readiness and time of which He is revealing to live from redemption even now.

The culmination of time required two aspects. As His Bride making Herself ready, our role was to surrender, surrender, surrender, surrender, and His role was to meet us at our surrender and take us higher into the Mind of Christ.

With the set time, there is no longer the two aspects. It is ONENESS. Basically what happened is we met and we ran into the culmination of time that placed us into the set time.

The set time consists of a oneness with HIM, where we are residing in the Mind of Christ and together we go higher and higher into Him. Higher into His vastness. Leaving the two aspects of our surrender on one end, combined with Him responding to our surrender, in exchange for our arrival at the culmination of time placing us IN HIM; and together we go deeper and higher into HIS VASTNESS as we await the SET TIME!

HE IS the set time and we are IN HIM as not only time, but we are IN HIM as THE SET TIME of the full manifestation of redemption coming forth, via being born again into the DNA of HIS existence!

How does this work? The better question is how do we live this?

We live, residing within and anticipating the set time by coming up higher. We live from the beautiful place of BECOMING REDEEMED rather than WAITING TO BE REDEEMED. We live from the higher ground of the reality that He is internal in these chosen vessels, taking them higher and higher and higher even now.

No longer living, thinking, breathing, surviving, making decisions, choices, or expecting outcomes from the fallen curse of mankind. But truly living from redemption of the fallen mind into the Mind of Christ, where everything is viewed and lived through the higher truth of original intention.

This is because HE is no longer moving into OUR lives. He is moving US into HIS Life. And as we view the fallen world we live in as already behind us....As we process everything from the Mind of Christ with the fallen mind already behind us......As we live and breathe and process and operate and view via the Mind of Christ and HIS original intention, it begins even now to change the dynamics of everything.

This is why we are sitting at the true location of...
ON YOUR MARK, GET SET, GO!

- **IT IS BECAUSE WE ARE ON THE MARK!**
- **WE ARE SET!**
- **AND IT IS TIME TO GO!**

A SET TIME!

LIVING, BREATHING, THINKING, OPERATING..... BECOMING REDEEMED EVEN NOW!

LIVING, even now from the full redemption of Christ the King of Redemption is the higher truth of 1 Thessalonians 5:23-24....

"Now may the God of peace Himself make all of you holy, completely, entirely, and may your whole spirit, and soul, and body be preserved blameless at the arrival of our Lord Jesus Christ. The One calling you is faithful, Who will also do it."

I am going to list that scripture again with some personal changes based on the move we are currently in which He is indeed currently making...

Now may the God of peace HIMSELF, Christ, THE KING OF REDEMPTION, make all of you, the entirety of each individual vessel, holy and redeemed. Completely and entirely redeemed. And may your whole being of spirit, soul, and body, be preserved blameless, without sin, redeemed to the original intention of the foundations of the Earth, at the INTERNAL arrival of our Lord, Christ the KING. For the one calling you is faithful. He will do this, and is in the process of actively and currently doing this!

His chosen and elite Navy Seal group of Bride has been in a process of individual, internal advancement in Christ the King but we are now in a corporate advancement, headed full on into Christ THE KING OF REDEMPTION. In revealing we are now in the corporate advancement because the move He is making has always been a corporate move... In revealing the advancement is now taking place as a corporate whole Bride rather than individual, He is showing us the beauty of everyone carrying equal weight. Within the corporate, it's not a matter of a wait lingering and lingering and lingering because this vessel is more ready, and now this other vessel has got to become more ready, and now this lagging vessel has got to catch up.

We have advanced beyond individual readiness into corporate readiness, where even though everyone within His corporate chosen elite vessels are still not all in the same level of readiness, the sum total of readiness is what He is looking at!

The sum total of the corporate readiness has produced the SET TIME and no longer the culmination of time!

This means fear and doubt can no longer hold back His chosen corporate. Any fear or doubt that arises is overcome IN HIM and the entire corporate continues to move forward!

THIS DOES NOT MEAN NO SPEC OF FEAR OR NO OUNCE OF DOUBT EVER SHOWS UP AGAIN. IT MEANS HE IS CONQUERING ALL DOUBT AND FEAR WITHIN THIS CORPORATE ADVANCEMENT.

OH, THE BEAUTY OF HIS HOLINESS!

This is an extravagantly beautiful example of how HE does the internal work because up until corporate advancement was possible in the reality of where we are, many individuals within the army of the mature and chosen Bride had a greater motivation of being set free from their personal captivity of fear than a greater motivation to govern with Him.

But within the corporate advancement we are now residing which includes going higher IN HIM as we RESIDE IN THE SET TIME, the motivation has drastically shifted from the craving to be set free of captivity into the love and excitement of governing and ruling and reigning with Him!

INDIVIDUAL READINESS BEING SOVEREIGNLY SHIFTED INTO THE POSITION OF CORPORATE ADVANCEMENT NOW TAKING PLACE HAS CHANGED THE DYNAMICS OF TIME!

THE BEAUTY OF CORPORATE ADVANCEMENT HAS ERASED US WAITING ON A CULMINATION OF TIME AND NOW HAS US WALKING STRAIGHT INTO A SET TIME WHEN CHRIST THE KING OF REDEMPTION WILL COMPLETE THE WORK OF REDEMPTION IN THE INTERNAL OF HIS CHOSEN, MATURE, ELITE BRIDE, COMING FORTH FROM THE VASTNESS OF WHO HE TRULY IS!

I am so in love with Him and everything He is doing in this process of the beautiful and sovereign move He is making deeper and deeper into the internal of HIS CHOSEN BRIDE!

Years ago He spoke, and said...***"I am removing fear from My Bride, for even My Bride has fear."***

He is doing it in His current, corporate move of redemption!

ON YOUR MARK!
GET SET!
GO!

NOTES

Chapter 4
THE BEGINNING OF TIMES!

He has already started the Beginning of Times.

His corporate Bride, led by His elite Bride, knowingly and unknowingly have absolutely stepped into the best of times ever lived since the fall of mankind in the garden with Adam and Eve. We are not waiting for Him to return for He is already here in the internal of the vessels who have been participating with Him in the sovereign move He announced on February 4, 2022 when He spoke and said, ***"I am about to make the move no one is yet aware of"***, then began revealing Himself to us and is now manifesting Himself within us with HIS LIFE growing much bigger than the seed of salvation. It is absolute truth to say, HE HAS COME...Rather than referring to *'WHEN HE COMES'*, as though it has not yet begun. **The title of this book is indeed, *'WHEN HE COMES'*, with the emphasis being on the coming forth of the FULL manifestation of Christ the King of Redemption in the internal of His vessels.** Which includes the molecular structure changes back to His DNA in the foundation of the Earth when He calls His sovereignly chosen vessels through His Bosom and passes them through the womb of the dawn of Psalm 110. That will truly be *'WHEN HE COMES'*. That will be when He releases His redeemed vessels into the Earth to rule and reign, hence the title, *'WHEN HE COMES.'*

However, to put the entire coming of Christ in the future is misleading, and not completely accurate because He is already here. HIS LIGHT HAS COME! He has already begun His sovereign move, and is already here on the Earth in a very tangible way, but also still a very hidden way. The only public awareness that He is already here while not yet the full manifestation of *'WHEN HE COMES'* has only been revealed or announced in the prior book *'THE BLIND DATE'*. Those He has already come to internally abide within, are still a very hidden group. But we can confidently and honestly say He has indeed come and it's not just a claim or a statement. We are experiencing outcomes and results because of His internal LIGHT coming forth!

With that said, much is taking place within the internal of the sovereignly chosen vessels. This is definitely not what most refer to as THE END TIMES.

It is the end of time as we know it. And when He sends these vessels back into the Earth, the end of an era will be over. The end of time as we have known it will be over. But the beautiful reality of what He is doing is not that He is bringing in THE END TIMES... the beautiful reality is, HE HAS ALREADY STARTED THE BEGINNING OF TIMES!

THE BEGINNING OF TIMES has begun unfolding and will continue to unfold until no one in the Earth will be able to deny what He has already started and will soon be making very, very public! With the title of this book being *'WHEN HE COMES'*, the reality is the entirety of this book is indeed speaking of the fulfillment of *'WHEN HE COMES'*, with everything within this book having already begun. What the world believes it is waiting on in regards to *'WHEN HE COMES'* has begun and will continue and will be fulfilled. This book is not to make a comprehensive list of things that will happen and what it will look like *'WHEN HE COMES'*. This book is to reveal deeper revelations that began *'THE BLIND DATE'* and continue in this writing of *'WHEN HE COMES'*. Overall, both books are sharing what it will be like *'WHEN HE COMES'* as well as what has already begun and what His coming is already looking like.

HE has already started manifesting more of His Life regarding the 'womb of the dawn' of Psalm 110, speaking of His Bosom. This is because He is bringing His Bride into perfect alignment of spirit, over soul, over body in the process of Her being born again as He spoke of in John 3 with Nicodemus. This 'womb of the dawn of the new day' of Psalm 110 is where the full molecular structure changes take place producing vessels not only full internally of His Life and His government, but also vessels of His Light whose DNA has been restored to the molecular structure of the DNA created in the foundations of the Earth. These Bridal vessels will return to carry forth the continuation of the beginning of times, having been changed and rearranged internally and physically. Distinct vessels of His Light, His Life, and His Love. Some of these vessels are already so deep in His Bosom they are already standing not only at, but within the menorah of the Sevenfold Spirits of God.

In 2017, He spoke to us and referred to the upper chamber of His Bosom being His womb. He spoke of how these chosen vessels, when returning would no longer recognize each other, nor would others recognize them for who they once were. They will be so completely changed as vessels carrying the fullness of Christ, His light, His love, and His voice of governmental authority, the physical molecular structure will be changed and no longer recognized. Their recognition will be based on His Life and His Light. When He spoke those things to us in 2017, He also said it would be a corporate creation. This work He would be doing, which He is now very actively doing, would be a corporate work. It is beautiful to now be able to say this is actively taking place not just with knowledge of being informed by Him, but with actual tangible evidence coming from the internal of these vessels of redemption already actively and actually taking place.

We are already experiencing as well as witnessing in each other so much internal redemption where the fallen mind is actively being restored and engaged with the Mind of Christ, it is beginning to show externally. These vessels are living day by day with tangible freedom, release of captivity, joy, peace, freedom, and a higher level of life IN HIM than ever before. These internal changes from Him residing with redemption in the internal place has grown to the degree it is evident in the external with the beginning of increased physical beauty, renewal of youth, and people witnessing His love coming through the eyes of others.

THIS IS BECAUSE IT IS HARVEST TIME! WHAT IS IN THE INTERNAL OF EACH PERSON IS CURRENTLY BEING HARVESTED!

WE ARE IN THE SEASON OF REAPING WHAT WE HAVE SOWN.

THE KINGDOM OF LIGHT AND THE KINGDOM OF DARKNESS ARE CURRENTLY PRODUCING HARVEST WITHIN THE PEOPLE OF THE EARTH. THE SEASON OF REAPING AND SOWING IS HERE. HARVEST OF LIGHT AND HARVEST OF DARKNESS IS COMING FORTH AND IS EVIDENT!

In the prior book, *'THE BLIND DATE'*, much was shared regarding KINGDOM SEPARATION. Kingdom separation takes place when it is harvest time. The harvest cannot take place without separation of the kingdoms. They go hand in hand. Harvest time is when His wheat is taken into the barn which is His Bosom of His presence where we go into Christ while He goes into us for the oneness that takes place in the process of redemption.

Kingdom separation and harvest time also includes the separation of Bridal, outer court, and those who will end up in hell. During kingdom separation those chosen for His Bosom have HIS INTERNAL LIFE of discernment of the tares. Tares are not discerned from the gift of discernment. Tares are discerned from the internal increase of His LIFE!

Kingdom separation, harvest time, and the discernment of the tares is all part of the evidence we are not standing in one position waiting for things to begin. Things have absolutely begun. It requires His internal Life in a mature state in order to be able to discern the tares. A vessel can have His Life, but if it's not mature enough, the tares are not discerned. But once

HIS LIFE INTERNALLY reaches a maturity level, the tares can be discerned. Until the moment a tare is discerned by a vessel of His mature Life, they look just like the others. They look just like us. The problem with a tare is their internal is the presence of darkness, whereas the internal of His mature Bride is the presence of His Life which is also His Light. He has made it very clear, a person is not a tare until they are discerned. Just like within His word, the tares grew with the wheat until there was a clear distinction within the head of the grain. The tare produces a different head, therefore it can be seen. It can be identified as a tare, representing the spiritual discernment.

This takes place AT HARVEST TIME! THE DISCERNMENT OF THE TARES TAKES PLACE AT HARVEST TIME!

TARES ARE ONLY DISCERNED BY WHAT HIS LIFE IN OUR INTERNAL DISCERNS IN THEIR INTERNAL. WE DO NOT DISCERN A TARE BASED ON THEIR ACTIONS, ALTHOUGH ACTIONS ARE THE ROTTEN FRUIT OF WHAT IS IN THE INTERNAL OF THE TARES. TARES ARE ONLY DISCERNED BY HIS LIFE IN THE INTERNAL OF THE MATURE BRIDE.

What He has recently begun showing is that once His Life in our internal has discerned the rotten internal of the tare, soon after we have discerned the internal as a tare, they display external rotten fruit on the outside which is a result of the internal darkness.

The point being, in the same way we are seeing external manifestations of the increase of His Life in the internal of His Bride such as mentioned above, we are seeing external manifestations of the internal darkness of the tares. Some examples would be extreme and dark mental torment, massive levels of confusion, increased levels of mockery, con work, manipulation, illnesses, and diseases from internal darkness which are displayed externally on the body or through the victim.

IN THE SAME WAY THE INTERNAL FLOWS TO THE EXTERNAL OF HIS LIFE IN THE BRIDE BRINGING FORTH HEALTH, VITALITY, YOUTHFULLNESS, BEAUTY, PEACE, JOY, HAPPINESS, WISDOM, PATIENCE, LOVE, AND SO MUCH MORE... THE INTERNAL DARKNESS OF THE DISCERNED TARES IS PRODUCING EXTERNAL DARKNESS.

It is highly important we have enough of the increase of the Life of Christ to discern the tares because this is a requirement of the manchild governing with the government of Heaven, governing our nation, and the church system. We are to not only govern our personal lives in order to separate ourselves from the tares, we are to govern them in the external as He leads. The bottom line is the tares are getting easier to discern because the increase of His Life in us discerning those vessels is a vital area of governing with the authority of Christ and of course it is a vital part of kingdom separation.

It is a dirty work we have to do. We must be willing to discern and identify the tares as extremely grievous as it is and remove ourselves from relationships with them.

As mentioned above, we are currently in active kingdom separation. Whatever the internal of a vessel produces is the identity of their personal harvest. These personal harvest create the corporate harvest on both sides of the track. Personal harvest produce corporate harvest of darkness and corporate harvest of the Kingdom of Christ of Redemption. **When the internal of a vessel is discerned and harvested, they are separated to the corresponding space based on their individual internal harvest of kingdom separation whether it be redemption, outer court, or the eternal darkness of hell.**

We are currently in the timeframe where the internal harvest is discerned, and also becoming visually evident through the things I just mentioned. We are becoming amazed at the vessels we are discerning who are currently in hell, although they have not yet passed away from this Earth. Their lives are displaying aspects of what we would call a living hell. Literally a living hell. Alive and LIVING, but experiencing the torment of hell without the eternal flames. Just as His chosen vessels are alive and living and experiencing the beauty of redemption although not yet taken to His Bosom and sent back through the womb.

The bottom line of what is taking place is that the Kingdom of God, His light, His love, the Life of Christ the King of Redemption is coming to a full manifestation in His chosen and ready vessels while at the same time the kingdom of darkness, deception, pride, the death of hell, is coming to a full manifestation in those already separated into the kingdom of hell.

We are still on Earth and we are manifesting Heaven. They are still on Earth and they are manifesting hell.

Two kingdoms are being harvested right before our very eyes and two kingdoms are being fully manifested right before our very eyes, and according to the traditions of men, we have not yet met what the church has called end times. This is because the SOVEREIGNLY CHOSEN VESSELS, WHICH IS A MANDATORY STEP AND REQUIREMENT OF THE PROCESS OF REDEMPTION, HAVE ALREADY BEEN CHOSEN AND ARE WELL ON THEIR WAY TO BEING REDEEMED WHILE STILL WAITING ON WHAT MOST ARE CALLING THE SECOND COMING OF CHRIST.

HE IS HERE, HALLELUJAH! HE IS HERE, AMEN!

AND WHEN HE FULLY COMES, EVERYONE WILL KNOW IT.

EVERY EYE WILL SEE!

WHEN HE FULLY COMES AND FINISHES THE MOVE HE IS ACTIVELY MAKING, THE FOLLOWING THINGS WILL BE EVIDENT TO EVERYONE NO MATTER WHICH KINGDOM THEY HAVE BEEN HARVESTED INTO...

- The Fear of the Lord will be the first of the Sevenfold Sprits manifested in the Earth.
- Youth will be restored in every vessel of redemption, not just this first chosen who are bringing this into fruition.
- The past will be removed.
- Memories will be removed.
- The redeemed will no longer be recognized, but they will be known with His identity.
- Our nation will be the home of His vessels of Light.
- The redeemed will operate in oneness with Christ the King of Redemption.
- His LOVE will do more than we ever thought His power would do!
- His redeemed will be sought out by the desperate.
- THE CAPTIVES WILL BE SET FREE!
- Families will be restored!
- Minds will be healed and made whole.

- THE REDEEMED OF THE LORD WILL HAND OUT HIS LOVE AND HIS REDEMPTION OVER AND OVER. THEIR SUPPLY OF LOVE AND REDEMPTION TO HAND OUT TO OTHERS WILL NEVER RUN DRY. IT WILL BE MULTIPLIED. AS THEY HAND OUT LOVE AND REDEMPTION TO ONE PERSON, THEY WILL TURN AND HAVE A BIGGER SUPPLY TO HAND OUT TO ANOTHER. THERE WILL BE A MULTIPLICATION OF HIS REDEMPTION! WHICH IS A MULTIPLICATION OF HIS LIFE IN THE EARTH!

- The fallen, unredeemed mind will not be able to comprehend or tolerate the Mind of Christ and the Mind of Christ will not be able to tolerate the fallen mind. They do not go together. But those with the Mind of Christ will carry others into redemption.

- As His chosen vessels of redemption carry redemption to others, they will also govern the Earth. For all of creation currently moans and groans for the manifested sons of God who are His vessels of redemption to govern the Earth. (Romans 8) The physical Earth. ALL OF CREATION IS TO BE AN EXTENSION OF HIM. Not just humans, but all of creation is to be an extension of Him!

It is important to point out WE HAVE NEVER BEEN THIS WAY BEFORE and new understandings of His manifested revelations are coming forth each day. There is no way enough books can be put together to keep the corporate Bride in total cadence with Him unless She has chosen to completely surrender Her existence and jump into cadence with Him. Yes, He has those who are chosen to be the very first! But overall redemption is for His entire Bride! When She has a hello moment with His Life in Her internal and jumps into cadence with Him, He will grant Her the opening of the Mind of Christ and She will catch on and catch up with what He is doing!

The war in Heaven is currently taking place which means soon and very soon there will be manifestation and a bursting forth of what we have already referred to as His Set Time.

1 Corinthians 15:46 reveals to us there is a natural before the manifestation of the spiritual. The cadence Christ is currently in involves the beginning of the Kingdom of God being handed back to God! In the natural the kingdom has been handed back to God with redemption currently manifesting in His first group of chosen vessels. In the spirit the war of Heaven is being fought over the spiritual kingdom of darkness CURRENTLY being handed back to the true spiritual Kingdom of God. (1 Corinthians 15:24)

Don't let the havoc satan is causing on the Earth or within your mind or life cause you to think the kingdom is not being handed back to God. It is actively being handed back to God via the Manchild, via the redeemed of the Lord already LIVING on this Earth while waiting the last manifestation of the complete fulfillment of redemption.

THE KINGDOM IS ABSOLUTELY CURRENTLY BEING HANDED BACK TO GOD BECAUSE THE KINGDOM OF GOD IS WITHIN. WITHIN. WITHIN. TAKE YOUR EYES OFF THE EXTERNAL.

THE KINGDOM OF GOD IS......... WITHIN!

THE FULL HANDING BACK OF THE KINGDOM IS WHEN WE ARE FULLY REDEEMED. THINK ABOUT IT! AS HIS CORPORATE BRIDE, WITH HIM STARTING WITH THESE "FORERUNNERS TO THE FORERUNNERS", THE FIRST ELITE GROUP OF BRIDE... WHEN THEY ARE FULLY REDEEMED AND HAVE COME FORTH THROUGH HIS WOMB, THAT IS WHEN THE KINGDOM HAS BEEN HANDED FULLY BACK TO GOD. AS THIS SOVEREIGN GROUP OF THOSE FIRST CHOSEN COME BACK AND CARRY THE MULTIPLICATION OF REDEMPTION

TO HIS WAITING AND DESPERATE BRIDE, IT WILL BE BECAUSE THE KINGDOM HAS BEEN HANDED BACK TO GOD.

YES AND AMEN!!

WHEN WE REALLY UNDERSTAND INTERNALLY WITH THE MIND OF CHRIST, THAT REDEMPTION TAKES US BACK TO THE ORIGINAL INTENTION IN THE FOUNDATIONS OF THE EARTH AND RESTORES US TO THAT ORIGINAL INTENTION, IT IS EVIDENT THAT IS WHEN THE KINGDOM IS HANDED BACK TO GOD! AND IT IS CURRENTLY HAPPENING......

WITHIN HIS CHOSEN VESSELS......

BECAUSE THE KINGDOM OF GOD IS WITHIN!

The war in Heaven is being fought over the kingdom being handed back to God, but we are almost totally there!

'WHEN HE COMES' IS ACTUALLY PAST TENSE, PRESENT, TENSE, AND FUTURE TENSE...

FOR HE HAS COME WITH REDEMPTION IN THE INTERNAL OF HIS FIRST CHOSEN VESSELS. HE IS PRESENT BECAUSE THE INTERNAL REDEMPTION IS INCREASING AND GROWING. AND THE FINAL FUTURE TENSE OF 'WHEN HE COMES' IS JUST AROUND THE CORNER WHEN THESE VESSELS COME BACK FULLY REDEEMED EXTERNALLY IN THE PHYSICAL BODY, AS WELL AS THE VERY CURRENT AND VERY ACTIVE INTERNAL REDEMPTION ALREADY TAKING PLACE!

Internal redemption is taking place because His Bride is so close to the womb of Psalm 110, the Womb of the New Day, the womb which is the upper chamber of His Bosom that she has stepped into and is standing inside the menorah, the Sevenfold Spirits of God.

AT THIS POINT, I AM GOING TO SHARE SOME UTTERANCES THE FATHER HAS SPOKEN TO US OVER THE YEARS. THERE HAVE BEEN WAY TOO MANY TO LIST IN THIS BOOK SO I HAVE CHOSEN A FEW THAT SHOW US HOW HE SPOKE YEARS AGO, BUT NOW HE IS FULFILLING WHAT HE SPOKE.

THIS SOVEREIGN MESSAGE OF THE MOVE HE IS MAKING BACK TO THE FULL REDEMPTION OF HIS ORIGINAL INTENTION OF THE MIND OF CHRIST IN THE FOUNDATION OF THE EARTH IS HARD FOR THE FALLEN MIND TO COMPREHEND.

I FIND IT VERY EXCITING AND ENCOURAGING HE SPOKE THINGS YEARS AGO HE IS CURRENTLY DOING. THIS SHOWS US EVERYTHING BEING SHARED IN *'THE BLIND DATE'* AS WELL AS *'WHEN HE COMES'* IS INDEED TRUTH, AND IS INDEED HAPPENING!

In 2016 He spoke to us in a word we titled SONG OF SONGS and said...

- ***"My Bride wears the menorah. She wears it with might! With the might of the Sevenfold. She has a date with the menorah. I am calling Her to Me for a date with the menorah to court Her and woo Her right into My throne. Her very being (the internal) shall be the authority of the menorah. She shall walk in the governmental authority of the menorah for these seven candles shall burn brightly within her!"***

Also in 2016 He spoke another word to us we titled CHECKMATE.

- A small portion of that word included where He spoke and said, ***"light and darkness will be on equal playing fields and then I will call checkmate and I will call My Bride to My Bosom!"*** (That will be the manifestation of Revelation 12 when the manchild is caught up to His throne)

In 2018 He spoke to us a word we titled THE WHEAT AND THE TARES...

- The word included Him telling us, ***"I planted you in my womb with my DNA to overcome!"*** **He also stated...** ***"As 1000 fall at your side and 10,000 at your right hand, it will not come near you, but you will see the tares fall around you."*** (This shows the large quantity of tares the internal Life of Christ in His redeemed Bride will be discerning)

In 2015 He spoke a word we titled ANANIAS AND SAPPHIRA...

- The word included Him telling us a veil will be removed. He also said, ***"many of you will walk in the court of Heaven to govern things, to rearrange things, to line things up, and to carry forth My authority, and when My gavel comes down, do not get in the way! I am stripping pride from My chosen, for I am taking My chosen higher, and I do not want it to cost them their life!"***

Another word from 2016 was given by the angel Gabriel. He stated...

- **"There has been a Holy exchange, I come to announce change, the black books are the redeemed prophets eating of Him, these are the Revelation 10:10 prophets. The elite of His Bride. Some words will settle bitter to the listener, and some words will be sweet to the listener. The return of My Son will not be secret. It will be violent. The closer He gets to the Earth within His redeemed,**

the more the chaos will increase." (I will add here. He is already increasing in His first group of redeemed, which means the closer He is getting to the Earth within His redeemed, and chaos is indeed increasing in our nation).

Another word from 2017 we titled I SEE MIGHTY CEDARS FALLING.

- It contained phrases that included ***"there will be casualties of war among you. For some will push the ballot. Some will remain to walk in wicked ways. Some will remain to walk in pride and stiff of neck and rebellion. The violent reaping of the wheat and tares has begun."***

He spoke to us in 2015. In a word we titled WATER TO WINE.

- In the word He spoke of transfiguration, transformation, and His manifested sons.

Another older word from Him in 2016, we titled EAGLES ARE SOARING.

- This Word spoke of Mount Zion. It said, ***"Mount Zion, (which is Christ), is about to be revealed for the day of reckoning is at hand."*** The word ended with the statement of. ***"THERE IS A SOON COMING TIME WHEN MAN'S REPENTANCE WILL MEAN NOTHING TO GOD!"***

  That statement remained a mystery to me for a long time, but I now understand with the kingdom separation spoken of in *'THE BLIND DATE'*. Once Christ the King separates people still living on Earth into their perspective kingdoms, those still alive on the face of the Earth whom He has already placed in the kingdom of hell, will try to cry out in repentance. However, that will be the time when "man's repentance will mean nothing to God." Unknowingly due to their own actions, choices, self will, and pride they have already been placed by His sovereign hand into the kingdom of hell although still living on the Earth.

On December 31st of 2016, New Year's Eve preceding New Year's Day of 2017. He spoke a word we titled CROWNS WILL BE STOLEN.

- There was a lot in that word, but it began by Him saying, **"I am coming to judge complacency. Most think I am coming to judge much bigger and greater, and I am, but I am beginning by coming to judge complacency."** I am, including that portion of the word because complacency means to not be aware. Not aware of what He is currently saying and doing. The above word regarding the soon coming time when man's repentance would mean nothing to God, is a perfect example of complacency because mankind is not aware that we are currently in a kingdom separation. Mankind is not aware the harvest has begun. That's the complacency God said He was coming to judge. He is currently judging complacency by separating the kingdoms, and people are completely clueless as to what HE is doing. THE CHURCH AS A WHOLE is not aware we are in God's Kingdom separation, and that His harvest has begun. That's complacency. And the complacency of not being aware of such a very vital time would put man in a place of finding that his personal repentance means nothing to God. THIS IS VERY GRIEVOUS, BUT VERY REAL AND IS CURRENTLY HAPPENING!

July 1st of 2017 we have a word that did not have a title, but it spoke of His Love.

- It said His Love will release the molecular structure that will change everything. It said His Love will set the captives free. It included that as we stand as His vessel with His Love internally, we will see the very molecular structure of the captive change right before our very eyes! It said His love IS HIS DNA, which is HIS molecular structure that will change everything!

In 2019 He spoke a word we titled I AM COMING TO VINDICATE MY NAME .

- In the word He said, ***"for MY LIGHT has come into the world to identify the wicked and to set the captives free."*** The word continued to say, ***"for Jacob I have loved and Esau I have hated."*** He repeated the word **'separation'** 15 times within the word He spoke, and then He said, ***"for the profane can no longer live with the holy, the profane must be removed! The profane can no longer be allowed to be with the holy, the profane must be removed!"***

2016/2017 we had the word from the Lord we titled CROWNS WILL BE STOLEN, which I referenced a portion of above from New Year's Eve 2016/New Year's Day 2017. .....

- This word also spoke of upheaval coming to the illuminati. He said, **"they thought they had perfect unity, but I am about to bring upheaval that will catch them by surprise."** The word said, **"they will think they have the upper hand, but I have a plan that will catch them by surprise!"** I believe we see that happening even now although the hidden work He is currently doing is still very hidden. It is about to be announced from Heaven! And it ABSOLUTELY WILL INDEED CATCH THEM BY SURPRISE!

In 2021 He spoke a word we titled SEVEN EYES AND SEVEN THUNDERS.

- This is a portion of that word... ***"I am releasing a new time, not a new season but a new time. I have released seven***

eyes to search the whole Earth to and fro. These eyes are the Seven Spirits of God and they shall search the whole Earth and they shall possess those whose hearts are made ready for God. The seven thunders, you shall speak with the seventh thunders, and this will come with violence. When I release My Son in a violent way, it shall come at a violent time. Remember Lot's wife, and do not look back! You shall release judgments as never before says Holy God. For I am releasing a destruction to trample upon deception!"

In 2018 He released a word we titled THE KINGDOM OF GOD IS VIOLENT.

- Some of this word included what He has been doing the last four years when He said He was about to make the move no one is yet aware of. Then He told us it was the blind date to get to know the vastness of Him. Before we knew that, He spoke this word which stated...... ***"I am going to take you to the foundations of the Earth and release fresh revelations of My Son not yet revealed. There will be a severing and a cauterizing of deceptions from the soul removing deceptions and limitations of My Son so that you can walk in the pure, unrevealed truth of My Son. These revelations of My Son will change your conversations."*** He continued to speak in the word of how He would take us into a time of getting to know His vastness, which is what He began when He announced the current sovereign move! THIS WORD IS ACTIVELY PLAYING OUT IN A VERY TANGIBLE WAY!

An older word from 2014 was titled THE CREATED MIND OF GLORY...

- It spoke of restoring the mind He created in glory in the foundations of the Earth. He spoke of removing our fallen mind and replacing it with HIS Mind, the Mind of Christ! That was 2014 and He began replacing the fallen mind with the Mind of Glory, the Mind of Christ in 2022. He is almost finished with that process and this first elite group of His Bride will soon be bursting forth into the Earth for the SECOND COMING OF CHRIST IN THE INTERNAL OF HIS VESSELS!

IN MARCH 2024, HE BEGAN TALKING TO ME ABOUT OUR NATION, THE UNITED STATES OF AMERICA.

- He began the conversation by speaking to me and saying ***"do not touch the oil and the wine."*** This comes from Revelation Chapter 6, and I had always believed the oil and the wine were His Bride. As I pondered Him bringing forth in my internal the statement of ***"do not touch the oil and the wine"***, I began to ponder the truth He was sharing of "do not touch my Bride". As I began to ponder, He spoke to me again and said... ***"Do not touch the redeemed!"*** I knew then the oil and the wine are the REDEEMED of the Lord we have spoken of throughout the entire book *'THE BLIND DATE'* as well as thus far in this book of *'WHEN HE COMES'*. He was letting me know, **"do not touch the oil and the wine"** is **"do not touch the redeemed of the Lord!"**

  The next thing He spoke was, **"do not touch America!"** I heard that so clearly in my internal, I questioned Him by asking, what? And He said, "***do not touch America, the land of the oil and wine, the land of the redeemed!"***

  "Do not touch the oil and the wine. The land of the redeemed! Do not touch the redeemed, America, the land of oil and wine! Do not touch America, the land of the redeemed!"

That was all He had to say in that moment, but it was enough!

The excitement in my internal was off the chain. Over the following months, He shared more with me about the vital importance of readiness in preparation of the small, sovereign group of His elite Bride and His purposes of not only sending Her back into the Earth to govern with the Sevenfold Spirits of God, but His divine will to begin spreading redemption in the nation of America!

This entire process of the move He is making that we are becoming day by day more and more aware of has been an extremely logic defying move. Everything He has said and done has defied logic because the fallen mind is logic, and He is defying, destroying, annihilating the fallen mind of man to be replaced with the redeemed Mind of Christ. With that being said, this internal move has been a logic defying move and one of the next things He spoke to me regarding our nation is... ***"if you continue to believe My words that defy logic, you will not need the food I once told you to prep and store. I will catapult you to the bosom for the sake of your nation!"***

Another time he asked me... ***"Are you willing for me to devastate you instead of your nation?"*** And because He had already given me and others such a large portion of His heart at that point, of course we answered Him with a resounding yes! We thought devastate meant we would be emotionally crushed. But in time He showed us that being willing to be devastated meant we were willing for Him to remove our total existence of who we have always been and who we currently are, and replace our existence with HIS existence of HIS DNA, HIS original intention, HIS mind of glory, HIS vessels of redemption!

He spoke to us regarding the process we had been in of how we once lived only out of the fallen mind from the curse of the fall of mankind our entire lives because that's all we had to work with. Then He began the process of removing the fallen mind and replacing it with the Mind of Christ. As beautiful as that has been, it has been hard. He spoke to us and said, ***"if you had stayed where you were, or even if you stay where you are, your nation will need the food stored up for hard times. But as you continue to go with Me where we are going, you will no longer need the food."*** I want to clarify here that He has made it very clear He's not saying there will absolutely not be any need for food or hard times in our nation before He turns our nation completely around into the land of the redeemed. He is saying as each vessel becomes redeemed, no matter what is going on around them they will no longer need the food, even if others around them are needing the food. Redemption is redemption. Redemption redeems us from the devastation and any potential need for food within our nation. When He said, "apply this to your nation", what He was saying is that anyone in our nation, (because America is the nation He is sovereignly choosing to begin His move of redemption within), anyone in our nation who believes His words that defy logic, will also not need the food. By continuing to move forward with Him and redemption, we will not need the food no matter what upheaval is going on around us!

- WE ARE NOT WAITING ON THE END OF TIMES.
- WE ARE LIVING THE BEGINNING OF TIMES!
- WE ARE NOT WAITING ON THE SECOND COMING OF CHRIST TO REMOVE US.
- WE ARE LIVING THIS SECOND COMING OF CHRIST ALREADY DWELLING WITHIN US!
- AND ANYONE WHO WILL BELIEVE THE LOGIC DEFYING WORDS IN 'THE BLIND DATE', AS WELL AS 'WHEN HE COMES', WILL ALSO BE REDEEMED UNTO HIS ORIGINAL INTENTION OF CREATION TO CARRY THE VASTNESS OF

WHO HE IS. FIRST OF ALL TO AMERICA, AND THEN TO THE REST OF THE WORLD BECAUSE HE PROMISES TO GIVE US THE NATIONS UNTIL THE ENTIRE EARTH HAS BEEN REDEEMED!

In order for Him to fully have His way, we must be willing to go on the blind date with Him and get to know who He truly is while not being offended or allow Him to move us past offense, and let Him annihilate the deceptions wrapped around the truth of who He truly is.

We cannot keep digging the same ditch and expect different results for His people, our families, us individually, our communities, our churches, our nation, or even the world. We have been doing the same thing over and over, but with different twist along the way and the state of the church, individuals, and this nation has only grown worse and deeper, into a deeper and darker hole of demise. When we are willing to quit digging the same ditch and let Him challenge and offend us into who He truly is, and how He is truly doing things in a way that defies logic, things will begin to change.

Any old wine skin has been an external method to bring His Life into the new. But it never has worked. We are now moving forward in the internal with His LIFE. This produces beautiful freedom IN HIM without the need for any old wine skins, old external methods, or ditches dug.

It's time to dance like David, unashamed, no matter what others think, and let Him offend us into the truth of WHO HE REALLY IS, CHRIST, THE KING OF REDEMPTION!

CONTINUE LORD, CONTINUE!

NOTES

Chapter 5
THE GREAT EXCHANGE.

There is a new sheriff in town and His name is <u>Christ the King</u> of Redemption.

HE IS RESTORING US UNTO THE RICHNESS OF WHO HE TRULY IS, HIDDEN IN THE VASTNESS OF HIS LIFE WE HAVE NEVER KNOWN!

There is a magnificently wonderful and beautiful exchange currently taking place in the elite group of His ready Bride, where understandings from the fallen mind are replaced with HIS KNOWINGS from the Mind of Christ. Understanding comes from the fallen mind of intellect, and knowing what HE KNOWS comes from the vastness of the Mind of Christ. In this process of exchange, believing what He is indeed currently doing overrides all understanding. Believing the vastness of the Mind of Christ He is releasing is where the victory lies. The victory does not lie in understanding from the fallen mind. The victory lies in believing the knowings of the Mind of Christ He is releasing to His Bride.

THE GREATEST EXCHANGE IS WHEN HE INCREASES HIS LIFE IN OUR INTERNAL AND FALLEN UNDERSTANDING IS REMOVED, WHILE KNOWINGS FROM THE MIND OF CHRIST INCREASE, AND INCREASE, AND INCREASE, AND INCREASE! THE GREAT EXCHANGE IS THE EXCHANGE OF FALLEN UNDERSTANDING FOR INCREASED KNOWING OF THE MIND OF CHRIST. WHILE ALSO EXCHANGING THE ANALYTICAL MIND FOR BELIEVING WHAT HE IS DOING EVEN WHEN WE DO NOT HAVE EXPLANATIONS.

OUR INDIVIDUAL VICTORY LIES IN BELIEVING WHAT HE IS SAYING AND DOING MORE THAN UNDERSTANDING WHAT HE IS SAYING AND DOING.

If we were keeping a calendar with Christ, the current event highlighted on the calendar would be the eve of the wedding coinciding with war at the edge of breakthrough. His Life takes us higher above the spiritual war, and we are able to live in His Life and Light of the higher ground of the Mind of Christ. We are locked in and protected while at the same time walking into His cadence of being chosen and placed at the wedding table. He has invited us to come up higher with Him. Higher above all things and more than anything, higher above the fallen mind and deeper into the Mind of Christ. In this place of being locked in and in the location of being higher in His Mind, the corporate Bride is stepping into a CORPORATE ONENESS. Not simply limited to being chosen as part of the corporate, but melding into oneness of the corporate where each and every individual Bride is in oneness with each other and Him! A oneness of the Groom and His individual Bride. We corporately fight together, we corporately go higher together, and we corporately know each cadence as it changes and how to navigate that cadence. We are corporately united with Him as one in our seeing, hearing, knowing, and walking out the voice of His Life without being alerted by another Bridal vessel. **We become alerted of the united awareness of knowing what HE is saying and doing when we realize we are operating in the same Life breath, which is a CORPORATE LIFE BREATH!**

WHILE ALL ALONG, WE CORPORATELY BELIEVE WHAT HE IS SAYING AND DOING!

WE BELIEVE!
WE BELIEVE!
WE BELIEVE!

He currently has appropriately raised us higher above the war of Heaven, where we are abiding in redemption even now. Our physical bodies are not yet redeemed into the DNA of the original intention of HIS CREATION, but our minds are gaining ground day by day and within each moment of living in the truth of redemption even now that brings joy, peace, rest, and knowing what He is doing in the same timing and cadence in which He is doing it. **We are realizing this sovereign corporate oneness is the true reality of "*the Kingdom of***

***God is violent and the violent take it by force."* The violence which takes the Kingdom of God by force is a corporate violence and a corporate force that can only reside in redemption and come forth from His Life of Redemption.**

The corporate Bride, the elite of His entire Bridal company, is daily becoming more one with Him, and more one with each other, which raises us higher into His Bosom and into the womb of the dawn of the New Day of Psalm 110. **There will be, very soon, a day of reckoning where the set time of redemption in which we are currently resigning, will burst forth through the womb of the dawn and His Bride will return to the Earth, dressed in the Holy array of HIS DNA, carrying the government of Heaven on Her shoulders, to rule and reign with Him!**

AS THIS ONENESS INCREASES, THE REALITY OF THE ONENESS PRODUCES THE BELIEVING WHICH OVERRIDES ALL KNOWING FROM THE FALLEN MIND. COMING FORTH FROM THE ONENESS IS A TANGIBLE AND NEW LEVEL OF BELIEVING EVERYTHING HE IS SAYING AND DOING BECAUSE THE DOING HAS SHIFTED TO THE BECOMING!

AS WE BECOME LIVING VESSELS OF HIS LIFE, THERE IS NO DEBATE AGAINST ALL FALLEN UNDERSTANDING AND REASONING. BECOMING TRUMPS ALL UNDERSTANDING!

In the written word, He stated of Himself that He had no reputation. When in reality He had a bad reputation with the Pharisees and He had a righteous reputation with some as being the Son of God. **He spoke He was of no reputation because when He died on the cross the man, the physical body did not just die. He transitioned to a King we have not YET COME TO KNOW. He spoke He had no reputation because His Life was transitioning and evolving into Christ the King of Redemption, the vastness of who He TRULY IS.**

A reputation is what a person is known for. Jesus knew even then we did not truly know who He was when He walked the Earth, nor did we know Christ the King of Redemption who had not yet been revealed. Hence, no reputation because we never knew Him in the truth and vastness of who HE IS until currently in the unfolding AND REVEALING of Christ the King of Redemption. **He had no reputation in the past, but He is here now with a reputation of Life, Love, and Redemption!**

A reputation is what we are known for and we have never known Him for who He really is. The current reputation He is sovereignly allowing us to not only gain from the Mind of Christ, but to be equal participants with is the reputation of redemption unto original intention created in the foundations of the Earth. His original intention for us to be fully HIS vessels manifested on the Earth. To fully carry HIS Life, HIS Love, and HIS Government of Heaven. True vessels of Christ the King!

Although we are waiting on the full redemptive manifestation of the DNA of Christ in our physical bodies, we are not waiting on redemption. This is because the tide has turned. Nothing is the same on this side of the turned tide. We do not steward our walk and life with Him the same. We are now carriers of Christ the King. We are no longer followers of Jesus. On this side of the turned tide we go higher IN HIM and live even now from the benefits of redemption. We are to *"FORGET NOT ALL HIS benefits!"*

His Life is residing internally and increasing with every cadence we walk with Him. When He shows us something internally we must not waiver and we must not look at the external. For the external is where deception lies. We are to live from this moment forward in the completion of internal redemption and let it begin to flow and manifest outwardly. First and foremost in our oneness with Him, our oneness with the corporate Bride, and within our individual lives.

Redemption of family, redemption of relationships, redemption of health, redemption of the fallen mind, redemption of provision, redemption of everything the enemy has stolen! **But mainly redemption of the Life of Christ that supersedes and goes so much farther than the seed of salvation. We must remain in what His Life has revealed and breathed into the internal, or looking at the external will confuse and can even cause us to look back.**

Looking back is very detrimental at this point. We are to remember the warning Jesus spoke when He warned to ***"remember Lot's wife, and do not look back"!*** Looking back is not only looking at our lives and what we have built with our lives, it is looking back or outward at the external that will rob the progression of the internal.

THE MAIN LOOKING BACK WE ARE TO BE WARNED OF IS TO NOT LOOK BACK AT WHO HE WAS RATHER THAN WHO HE IS AND IS TO COME!

LOOKING BACK AT THE LIMITED JESUS OF NAZARETH RATHER THAN CONTINUING TO GO FORWARD WITH THE UNLIMITED CHRIST THE KING OF REDEMPTION IS THE LOOKING BACK WE ARE NOT TO TAKE EVEN THE SLIGHTEST GLANCE INTO.

He is not coming and filling the internal of those in love with self, those in love with religion, those in love with the church system, or those in love with Jesus of Nazareth. **He's coming to those in love with the fullness of The Way, The Truth, and The Life of Christ the King of Redemption! The man on the cross was and is finished. But Christ the King of Redemption is now here!**

He told us Himself on the cross that it was finished, and we have made that to mean so many things! But what was truly finished was and remains to be the finished EXTERNAL work of Jesus of Nazareth. And now we step into and live through the INTERNAL Life of Christ the King!

WHEN HE COMES, it begins in the internal. It is internal and it increases internally, cadence by cadence, oneness by oneness, before it comes out and manifest into the Earth.

WHEN HE COMES, HE IS INTERNAL BEFORE THERE IS OUTWARD EVIDENCE.

However, at this time there are those who are already experiencing the outward evidence. For the remainder of His corporate Bride beginning to step into the cadence of redemption, He will come first into the internal with the increase of the seed of Christ into the Life of Christ, and it will grow and increase, and grow and increase, until there is outward evidence of Christ the King of Redemption.

ALL THE WAY UNTIL THERE IS EXTERNAL EVIDENCE OF REDEMPTION TO THE CREATION OF ORIGINAL INTENTION!

We must become sensitive and remain sensitive to the higher truth that as we go deeper into Him in this process of redemption, we leave fallenness behind us! As He sovereignly takes us higher IN HIM and simultaneously as we stay in cadence with HIM, we are leaving more and more of our fallen lives and our fallen minds behind us. It is imperative we fix our mind on the Mind of Christ and not on things of this world or the fallen mind. The higher we go IN HIM, the higher we go into the Mind of Christ and more of our cursed fallen minds and fallen lives fall behind us! We leave fallenness behind! **He is telling us to live our lives to the fullest. When He does so He is not talking about living our fallen lives to the fullest because more and more of it is no longer even existing! He is talking about living life IN HIM as we are actively gaining**

and going higher IN HIM and living more fully in HIS LIFE!

CURRENTLY, HE IS SAYING IT'S NOT MUCH LONGER OF A WAIT UNTIL WE SEE HIM FACE-TO-FACE. DURING THIS TIME WE ARE TO LIVE FULLY IN HIM WHILE WE WAIT, A LITTLE BIT LONGER! WE ARE NOT TO WAIT IN THE FALLEN MIND AND FALLEN LIFE. WE ARE TO WAIT IN THE HIGHER GROUND OF THE MIND OF CHRIST FOR A LITTLE BIT LONGER!

We have a role to play with taking our thoughts higher, our conversations higher, our beliefs higher, and the way we process our daily lives. Making the deliberate choice to go higher in our thoughts, our decisions and our conversations. That's our part! The other aspect of going higher is sovereign and comes from Him.

At times we will tangibly feel Him internally take us higher and at other times we become more and more aware of an increase of His Life, as well as an increase of internal peace because He has sovereignly taken us higher. He is currently corporately taking us higher with a very sovereign cadence completely outside of our making and doing! **Combined with His invitation for us to go higher, this includes aspects we can initiate with our choices, decisions, and what we set our mind upon, combined with the beautiful and sovereign aspect that only comes from Him. Yet they go hand in hand perfectly.**

We are to BELIEVE HIM when HE tells us it's not much longer, even though not much longer to Him could and most likely is different than what that means to us. We are to remain excited and encouraged that He loves US so much HE is encouraging us by informing us it's not much longer until full REDEMPTION comes forth. We have the authority IN HIM to take our thoughts, our conversations, and our decisions higher. Within His sovereign role where He reaches internally and sovereignly takes us higher in this move He is indeed making, drawing us closer and closer to the checkmate of full redemption, we are to celebrate, celebrate, celebrate our life in Him as it grows and increases in the beautiful oneness between us and Him. Between us and the corporate Bride internally with Him!

THIS MEANS THAT WHILE LIFE IS NOT PERFECT AND STILL HAS STRUGGLES, HE IS EQUIPPING US WITH THE STRATEGY OF HIS LIFE TO GO HIGHER ABOVE EVERY PROBLEM AND STRUGGLE! WHEN WE HIT A BUMP IN LIFE, HE IS EQUIPPING US WITH HIS INTERNAL LIFE TO SHIFT OUR FOCUS FROM THE CURSED FALLEN MIND INTO THE HIGHER GROUND OF THE MIND OF CHRIST!

IT SOUNDS LIKE A MENTAL TASK, BUT IT HAS BECOME A SMOOTH AND SILKY SOVEREIGN BLESSING FROM CHRIST THE KING!

WE ARE CURRENTLY LIVING SUCH A DIFFERENT MINDSET. IT'S A MIND, SET ON HIM! A VERY TANGIBLE DIFFERENCE OF INTERNAL REDEMPTION RAISING US HIGHER THAN THE FALLEN LIFE WE HAVE ALWAYS BEEN AWARE OF.

The bottom line is that as we go higher, we are governing. As we go higher, we are governing the Kingdom of God, people, circumstances, situations, and even things pertaining to our nation.

WE ARE IN A VERY STRATEGIC TIME! WE ARE NOT MERELY PLUGGING ALONG AND SURVIVING, EVEN WHEN THINGS ARE VERY HARD. WE ARE GOVERNING EXTREMELY HIGH LEVEL THINGS SUCH AS HANDING THE KINGDOM BACK TO GOD AND NOW THAT IT'S IN HIS HANDS NATURALLY, AND THE WAR OF HEAVEN IS TAKING PLACE SPIRITUALLY, WE ARE ACTIVELY GOVERNING PEOPLE, SITUATIONS, CAPTIVITY, AND SITUATIONS WITH OUR NATION AS WE GO HIGHER IN HIM!

CHRIST, THE KING IS VERY AWARE. EXACTLY AWARE. SPECIFICALLY AND WITHOUT ERROR, AWARE OF THE HEART OF MAN.

HE IS FULLY AWARE AS TO WHO IS TAKING A CHANCE ON HIM AND BELIEVING EVEN WHEN THERE IS NOT FULL KNOWING OF WHAT HE IS ACTIVELY DOING IN THIS SOVEREIGN MOVE OF REDEMPTION.

THIS IS BECAUSE TRUE BELIEVING AND TAKING A CHANCE ON HIM, INVOLVES CHANGE AND ACTION NOT LIMITED TO SIMPLY CLAIMING WE BELIEVE!

BELIEVING MOVES FROM THE HEAD, TO THE HEART, TO EXTERNAL CADENCE WITH HIM AND DOES NOT REMAIN IN THE FALLEN MIND OF MAN.

TRUE BELIEVING ONLY BEARS FRUIT WHEN IT IS BIRTHED FROM THE MIND OF CHRIST!

We are at a critical time when HE desires US to believe what HE is saying and doing, even when we cannot fully comprehend. As we believe, experiencing His Life fortifies us with the comprehension needed for what He is doing!

He is currently not only confirming things, He is actually doing them which is the clearest sign of how extremely close we are to full redemption and being the manifested sons of God all of creation is groaning for. We still do not know exactly when, but we are sitting on a time bomb of closeness no matter what that means to Him.

HE IS MAKING SURE WE ARE VERY AWARE OF THE MOVE HE IS ABSOLUTELY MAKING OF WHICH WE WERE ONCE NOT YET EVEN REMOTELY AWARE OF!

THE MORE WE SURRENDER ALL ANALYTICAL AND INTELLECTUAL UNDERSTANDING FROM THE FALLEN MIND OF MAN FOR THE GREAT EXCHANGE OF THE KNOWINGS OF THE MIND OF CHRIST RESIDING IN OUR INTERNAL, THE MORE WE BECOME HIS VESSEL......

HIS READY BRIDE!

He already knows who His corporate Bride is and within that corporate Bride, He already knows who is currently ready. We are not to let that disqualify us if we are not YET ready! We are not to try and understand from the fallen mind what that means. We are to get in cadence with Him and keep moving forward with the beautiful excitement of this sovereign move He is indeed making. Because plain and simple, He is getting us ready and as long as we are cooperating, He will continue to get us ready. It is His work because it is His sovereign move! And praise HIS HOLY NAME there are those fully ready who will very soon see the fireworks and the kickoff of this beautiful sovereign move HE is making that no one was once aware of, but some have now become very aware of and are about to be fully aware of!

Do not disqualify yourself just because you fear, think, or know you are not part of the elite FIRST group. Celebrate them! Pray for them! Seek them out! Learn from them! Encourage them! Cheer them on! Because in doing so you will gain the Life of Christ leading you into redemption even if it comes fully into you after the first group. The important thing is that it comes into you!

THIS FIRST CORPORATE GROUP OF HIS ELITE BRIDE, ALREADY LIVING THROUGH INTERNAL REDEMPTION AND ANXIOUSLY AWAITING THE VERY SOON FULL REDEMPTION OF HIS DNA HAVE BEEN THROUGH HELL AND BACK FOR YOU FOR DECADES. BE GRATEFUL!

AND CORPORATELY THEY SAY WITH ALL RESPECT, "YOU ARE WELCOME!"

His DNA is in you, whether you are just becoming aware of it or not!

THERE IS A NEW SHERIFF IN TOWN, AND HIS NAME IS CHRIST THE KING OF REDEMPTION. HE COMES WITH A POSSE OF A CORPORATE BRIDE, READY AND LOADED WITH THE AUTHORITY OF THE GOVERNMENT OF HEAVEN!

WHEN HE WAS JESUS OF NAZARETH, HE CAME AS SAVIOR. NOW HE IS OUR KING OF REDEMPTION. HE IS HERE! HE HAS COME AS OUR KING, THE RULER OF THE NATIONS!

We have been measured in the measurement of Him based on Ephesians 4, the full measure of Christ. And because of that full measurement, plumb lines are dropped into the lives of those who become associated with HIS READY BRIDE! Believe!! Connect!! Become part of HIS CORPORATE BRIDE!

EVEN NOW WITHIN HIS CORPORATE BRIDE, WE HAVE THOSE WHO ARE READY AND WAITING, THOSE WHO ARE QUICKLY IN THE PROCESS OF BEING READY, THOSE WHO HAVE STEPPED INTO THE READINESS PROCESS, AND THOSE WHO ARE JUST BEING INFORMED THEY ARE PART OF THIS SOVEREIGN AND AMAZING CORPORATE BRIDE.

The importance lies in knowing the truth of who you are! You are part of His corporate Bride. Let Him show you where you stand IN HIM and let HIM take you the rest of the way!

Even as you read this book and possibly also the prior book of *'THE BLIND DATE, THE MISSING LINK TO BRIDAL READINESS',* a plumb line of Christ the King is dropped into your life. There are some the Lord is protecting at this point from the plumb line of Christ. **These books are written for those He is preparing to send to those He is currently protecting.** It all defies logic from the fallen mind of man and fits beautifully in the internal from the Mind of Christ! **By this time of reading these books, you should know if you are on the team of those being prepared or the team of those being protected.**

Those on the team being prepared know to run to the front line and become focused. BECAUSE HE IS FAITHFUL AND TRUE. HE JUDGES AND MAKES WAR.

IT IS DOUBT THAT CAUSES US TO FLOW FROM LOGIC, BUT IT IS SURRENDER THAT CAUSES US TO STEP INTO BEING PREPARED!

WE ARE NOT TO BE WAITING ON HIM TO SEEK US OUT, WE ARE TO BE RUNNING IN CADENCE TO MEET HIM! HE IS COMING TO THOSE WHO HAVE TURNED AND ARE STAYING TURNED FROM THEIR WICKED WAYS OF SELF-SUFFICIENCY IN EXCHANGE FOR THE LIFE OF CHRIST, THE ALL SUFFICIENT ONE!

As we finish this chapter, we are headed to the conclusion of this book where we will take a look at things Christ the King has revealed which will compose where we are headed, WHEN HE FULLY COMES.

There is no need for us to wonder or worry on either side of the coin as to what things are going to look like, sound like and actually be like. He is preparing us now in the internal of our beings for the pure beauty of things WHEN HE COMES. And we know we can trust Him with the rest when we are sent back to the Earth to rule and reign with HIM. We will be vessels of the full Mind of Christ, the full Kingdom of Heaven, the full knowing of Christ the King of Redemption.

1 Corinthians 15:22-28...
For as in Adam, all die, so also IN CHRIST shall all be BE MADE ALIVE. But each in his own order, Christ, the first fruits, THEN AT HIS COMING, THOSE WHO BELONG TO CHRIST. Then comes the end, WHEN HE DELIVERS THE KINGDOM TO GOD, (our redemption IN HIM), after destroying every rule and every authority and power. For He must reign until He has put all His enemies under His feet. The last enemy to be destroyed is death. God has put all things in subjective under His feet. But when it says, all things are put in subjection, it is plain that HE is expected to put all things in subjection UNDER HIM. When all things are subjected TO HIM, then the Son Himself will also be subjected to Him, and put all things in subjection under Him, that God may be ALL IN ALL.

THE ABOVE IS WHAT WE WERE CREATED FOR. THE ABOVE IS WHAT WE ARE CURRENTLY BEING CALLED INTO AND BEING EQUIPPED FOR. THE ABOVE IS WHAT HE IS ACTIVELY DOING IN HIS VESSELS.

GO DEEPER WITH HIM AND HIS CORPORATE BRIDE AS YOU READ THE REMAINING CHAPTERS OF SOME THINGS HE HAS REVEALED TO US OF WHAT IT WILL BE LIKE...

WHEN HE COMES.

NOTES

Chapter 6
LOOK UP, LOOK INTERNAL, BUT NOT OUT!

He is endless and limitless and His vastness is never ending.

Assuming you have read this far into the pages of *'WHEN HE COMES'*, and especially if you have also read the pages of *'THE BLIND DATE, THE MISSING LINK TO BRIDAL READINESS'*... it has been ingrained in you by now the importance of looking up for our redemption, looking internal where He is abiding and increasing His Life in us, and the dangers of looking outward into the physical where all deception resides.

This chapter is certainly not an exhaustive list including everything that is coming forth now or will come forth, WHEN HE COMES. In this chapter, you will be reading the majority of the things He has revealed thus far that will be taking place that glorious day we are waiting upon WHEN HE COMES!

Some of these things will just simply be listed, and some will be included with a brief description. The things being shared are going to start with the upheaval of WHEN HE COMES because when the vastness of His Life, His Light, and His Love come into the atmosphere of the physical Earth, the spiritual force is going to create great and massive upheaval! The upheaval will be widespread, deep, and devastating. The victory will lie in the return of His chosen vessels who will be the manifested sons of Romans 8, the deliverers of Obadiah 21, those who do the great exploits of Daniel 11, the manchild of Revelation 12, those carrying the full authority of the entire government of Heaven of the Sevenfold Sprits of God spoken of in Isaiah 11, the authority of the 144,000 in Revelation 14, those with a new name and a new song,...... THE REDEEMED OF THE LORD!

He will be sending His vessels of LIGHT, LOVE, and LIFE to trample upon deception, but also to govern and bring redemption to every area of upheaval.

HIS REDEEMED VESSELS WILL GOVERN FROM THE INTERNAL OF THEIR BEING. INTERNALLY, THEY WILL SEE AND UNDERSTAND FROM THE MIND OF CHRIST EXACTLY

WHAT NEEDS TO BE DONE AND HOW TO DO IT. ALL GOVERNMENTAL AUTHORITY OF HEAVEN WILL BE RESIDING IN THEIR INTERNAL AND ALL GOVERNING WILL COME FORTH FROM THE INTERNAL.

As I continue to speak of the upheaval, do not lose sight that He is starting with great turmoil in our nation as His introduction to what will be redeemed into what He has referred to as A WHOLE NEW WORLD, A NEW FANTASTIC POINT OF VIEW! AND WHAT HE HAS REFERRED TO AS HIS GREATEST SHOW ON EARTH!

REDEMPTION OF ALL THINGS UNTO HIS ORIGINAL INTENTION OF CREATION IN THE FOUNDATION OF THE EARTH. THE REMOVAL OF ALL FORMS OF DEFEAT, DECEPTION, AND DEATH WITHIN HIS CHOSEN, WHILE OTHERS CONTINUE TO REMAIN IN THEIR WICKED WAYS. WHILE THEY PACK THEIR BAGS AND FLEE OUR NATION, AND WHILE OTHERS FALL AT THE FEET OF HIS LIGHT AND JOIN HIS CORPORATE BRIDE OF REDEMPTION.

When we read John 3:19, we see that His Light comes into the Earth to judge the Earth. His Light is about to enter the Earth with such a degree it will look, feel, and smell like great defeat and destruction to those who do not have eyes to see and ears to hear what He is doing. Simultaneously with His destruction, will be His chosen vessels who have been internally equipped to turn everything around.

HIS ENTRANCE INTO THE EARTH WITHIN THE INTERNAL OF HIS CHOSEN BRIDE WILL NOT BE OVERLOOKED AND MISSED. IT WILL BE CLEAR, OBVIOUS, OVERWHELMING, FEARFUL, AND BEAUTIFUL.

It is easy to see HIS REDEMPTION OF ALL DESTRUCTION AND UPHEAVAL will take some time, but it will be a glorious time for

His chosen and for those who run to and seek out His chosen. It will be a horrific time for those who refuse His Light, His Life, and His Love.

He has revealed that the return of His chosen and equipped Bride will bring an Earthquake to our nation. He has not shared with me the degree of devastation this Earthquake will produce, but it will not be a slight incident.

There will also be great fire. In 2009 He spoke in what we referred to as 'His prophetic utterances' because His words spoke of Himself, and He said... ***"It will be no less than a tsunami of fire. It will be no less than a volcanic eruption."*** As to what is going to produce that type fire, I cannot say with absolute surety, but He did ask me a question during that timeframe of, ***"have you considered meteors coming into the atmosphere of your nation?"*** Perhaps that will be how the fire takes place.

During this horrible and tragic time, the chosen and equipped Bride........those these books are waking up, preparing, and equipping......will be completely and totally protected and untouched. They will literally live in a bubble of HIS LIFE protecting them from all things destructive and all things evil.

The natural disasters will produce a chain effect of upheaval in every system of our nation, including the economic system, political system, educational system, retail and supply system, infrastructure and travel of all kinds, and even the church system. There will be a literal civil war within the church between the religious who will not let go of the past and embrace what HE indeed is currently doing.

THE REJECTION OF CHRIST THE KING WILL BE NO LESS THAN THE REJECTION OF JESUS OF NAZARETH. THE RELIGIOUS WILL REJECT AND CALL IT OF HELL AND THE

DARKNESS WILL CALL IT HOLY!

His equipped Bride will be sent back to govern each area mentioned above. She will know from the full and internal Mind of Christ exactly how to govern and bring redemption to every area of our nation.

As I continue to share things He has revealed to us regarding THE WHOLE NEW WORLD, THIS NEW FANTASTIC POINT OF VIEW, AND THIS GREATEST SHOW ON EARTH OF HIM, HIS LIFE, AND HIS LIGHT, you will be reading repetitions of things included in *'THE BLIND DATE'* as well as in *'WHEN HE COMES.'* I am putting everything here again and adding to it as He reveals new truths. I believe it is important to make a comprehensive list all in one place to give us the impact of where we are headed with the emphasis being on total redemption back to the original intention of how He created things to be in the foundations of the Earth. Back to the very beginning. The beginning, of the beginning, of the beginning, of time! Back to His original intention before there was ever a fall of mankind producing the fallen and highly cursed mind of man.

MANKIND HAS COOPERATED WELL WITH THE FALLEN AND CURSED MIND OF MAN TO MAKE A MESS OF EVERYTHING. CHRIST THE KING OF REDEMPTION IS COMING TO BRING GREAT DESTRUCTION TO THE MASSIVE MESS MANKIND HAS MADE BEFORE HE REDEEMS IT ALL INTO THE PERFECTION OF HIS ORIGINAL INTENTION!

As we move forward, you will recognize most of these, and you will read of more He has revealed.

So let's continue........

💣 There will be the restoration of families. All brokenness and separation will be restored.

- Restoration of relationships outside of families. Those we are not related to.

- Memories of our prior existence will be removed as we operate in our new creation of His complete vessels!

- Most, if not all Bride returning into the Earth will be relocated and not placed back where they currently live. All relocations will be for His will to go forth as originally planned. You will not be lost and confused. You will know from the Mind of Christ exactly what He needs from you and your family.

- Marriages will truly be made in Heaven. Single people, whether never married, divorced, or widowed who are also His Chosen Bride will be placed with the spouse He originally created for them. People currently married to who God truly chose for them will also be married to a 'new person' because it will be the man or woman they were originally created to be and not who they knew them to be prior to redemption. Hence, truly marriages made in Heaven!

- Each redeemed person, whether in the original group of corporate Bride or those receiving redemption when the forerunner Bride returns, each individual will have the full authority of Christ operating internally when they step into redemption. THE FULL AUTHORITY OF CHRIST THE KING!

- Within the church system we will have the restoration of the apostle/prophet/teacher. Those leading the church and navigating the cival war of the church will not be operating in gifts. They will be operating in the Sevenfold Sprits of God, the Life of Christ, and the combined office of apostle/

prophet/teacher.

- Redeemed vessels will be operating in the full Sevenfold Sprits, governmental authority of Heaven with the authority to govern the Earth and every aspect of society to the creation of the original intention of Christ the King.

- Captives will be set free! We all have captivity of the fallen and cursed mind. The mind will be set free including all captivity of mental illnesses, disorders, sicknesses, struggles and dysfunctions. All physical disorders, diseases, curses, sickness and struggles including all forms of addiction, will be set free as redemption comes forth, including complete healing within the physical body.

- The nation of America will be redeemed and in the process of full redemption coming to our nation, He has spoken and said ***"I am going back to the declaration of independence, and I'm going to undo it all***"...

- This is because He has spoken clearly that even when upheaval is not fully restored, and even with evil and wicked people still being in our nation, even with much religion still in our nation, He is calling America, the land of the redeemed. This will be true because our government will be redeemed back to HIS original intention of the government of Heaven! That is a massive, heavy, beautiful, and exciting truth He has shared!

- With each redeemed vessel, their youth will be restored, aging, and all consequences of aging will be redeemed and death will be removed. DEATH WILL BE CONQUERED!

- Each redeemed vessel will internally live in the joy that comes in the morning, which is an expression of Him! HE IS THE JOY THAT COMES IN THE MORNING!

- We will live the reality of the restoration of the years the locust have eaten.

- The toil and sweat of the brow will be removed. Provision of the redeemed will be abundant and flowing.

- We will see the restoration of His true church without division of traditions of men, doctrines, theologies not of Him, opinions of man, religion, and all forms of separation.

- Isaiah 60 will be fulfilled.

- Isaiah 61:2-3 will come forth which states... ***'And the day of vengeance of our God'***, for redemption IS the day of vengeance. The remainder of that prophecy over Christ from verse 3-4 and onward will come forth via redemption!

- The Holy Spirit will be removed from the Earth. He will remain increased in His redeemed for the internal of the redeemed will house the Trinity of the Father, Christ the King, and the Holy Spirit.

- He will release the three generational blessing of Abraham, Isaac, and Jacob. Redemption is falling on families, and an example would be myself, my adult children, and my grandchildren, all being sovereignly included in this beautiful sovereign move of redemption.

- The former struggles and defeats will be removed from sight and not remembered or come to mind. Meaning not only the defeats and struggles removed, but also the memories of our past unredeemed defeats and struggles.

- We will see the fulfilling of Psalm 110, the redeemed of the Lord, dressed in His Holy Array which is the DNA of His blood, which is His love, which is His original intention of

LIFE for HIS chosen vessels.

- He has spoken, ***"the evil and wicked of our nation will think they have the upper hand, but I the Lord God have a plan that is going to catch down by surprise!"*** The plan that is going to catch them by surprise is redemption! Redemption of His chosen, who will bring destruction and death to the wicked and evil who think they have the upper hand. When we look at our nation, it is clear to see they do indeed have the upper hand, but God's sight and truth is that He has the upper hand and it's about to come forth in a very obvious way!

- People will no longer recognize the redeemed of the Lord, but they will know the redeemed of the Lord by their true existence of who they have become in Him and more so they will know them by the essence of Christ the King and HIS LOVE! We will be so hidden by HIS identity, HIS love, and HIS LIGHT, others will no longer recognize us! He has said ***"they will not recognize you, but they will know you!"*** This is because recognition requires memory, and the memory of who we once were will be removed, but they will know us for who we are now in Christ!

- All redeemed of the Lord will be vessels of His Light where others can literally see His Light coming forth.

- All redeemed of the Lord no matter what age will be in oneness of Christ the King and His corporate Bride.

- All redeemed of the Lord no matter what age will carry His Love. A love we have never experienced before which will change the molecular structure of whatever He stands us in front of. Whether this be a mountain to become a plain such as Zachariah 4. Or whether this be restoration from an Earthquake. Including the molecular structure of a captive individual. The molecular structure of the mind and the body will be changed right before our very eyes as HIS LOVE in our internal stands before the captives! **SOMEBODY SHOUT!!!**

- His redeemed will carry a love that will do more than we ever thought His power would do!

- There will be great separation of the kingdoms. Great separation of those whose repentance will mean nothing to God because it will be too late for them. We will experience a great separation of those who have chosen hell, the outer court, and the Bosom of God, the Redeemed of the Lord!

- The chosen will hand out His love to others and it will multiply greatly in others to now possess His Love internally and pass it on to even more people desperate for HIM.

HE IS ENDLESS AND LIMITLESS AND HIS VASTNESS IS NEVER ENDING!

WE HAVE ONLY JUST BEGUN TO LIVE FROM THE LIFE OF WHO HE IS AND NOT WHO WE THOUGHT HIM TO BE.

NO LONGER LIMITED!

We must not fail to look up, to look inward, and do not look out! The outward is the physical where all deception lies. As we grow more and more in the Mind of Christ, we will disconnect more and more from the outward physical deception and go deeper into THE KINGDOM OF GOD WITHIN!

NOTES

Chapter 7
THE POWERS OF THE AGE TO COME!

"They overcame him by the blood of
the Lamb and the word of
their testimony"

Plain and simple, yet while also simultaneously blowing the capacity of the fallen mind, **THE POWERS OF THE AGE TO COME, ARE THE SEVENFOLD SPIRITS OF GOD!** Each of these Spirits are expressed in the fullness of Christ the King of Redemption within the fullness of the government of Heaven. The Sevenfold Spirits come forth and are identified as THE POWERS OF THE AGE TO COME.

Hebrews 6:5 mentions the powers of the age TO COME, referring to a future age, a new era, not at the time of the writing of Hebrews. An age TO COME. With the emphasis of that verse being on POWERS waiting within that age to come. Not current powers. Not past powers, but powers on reserve for the age to come. Hence, the truth, the scripture, and the title of this chapter of, THE POWERS OF THE AGE TO COME!

WE ARE CURRENTLY IN THE TIME OF THE AGE TO COME BECAUSE THAT IS THE TIME OF REDEMPTION! THE AGE OF REDEMPTION WE ARE NOW BEING VERY MUCH MADE AWARE OF WHICH HE SPOKE OF ON FEBRUARY 4, 2022 WHEN HE SPOKE AND SAID, *"I AM ABOUT TO MAKE THE MOVE NO ONE IS YET AWARE OF."*

HE NOW HAS THOSE WHO ARE ACTIVELY BEING MADE VERY AWARE OF THE MOVE HE IS CURRENTLY MAKING THAT IS NO LONGER ON HOLD.

- THE MOVE OF REDEMPTION. THE MOVE OF THE AGE TO COME!

- AND THIS AGE TO COME IS AN AGE OF 'POWERS OF THE AGE TO COME!'

This chapter began by stating THE POWERS OF THE AGE TO COME ARE THE SEVENFOLD SPIRITS OF GOD. The Sevenfold Sprits of God are the complete government of Heaven, which rest on His shoulders, and which His chosen vessels will carry in the internal to govern, rule, and reign. Isaiah 11 reveals to us the Seven Spirits of God consist of:

1. **The Spirit of the Lord**
2. **The Spirit of Wisdom**
3. **The Spirit of Understanding (sometimes referred to as the Spirit of Revelation)**
4. **The Spirit of Council**
5. **The Spirit of Strength (sometimes referred to as the Spirit of Might)**
6. **The Spirit of Knowledge**
7. **The Spirit of the Fear of the Lord**

Each of these seven spirits residing in Christ the King and now residing in His ready Bride, are the powers from which the age to come will be manifested.

Equally so, THE POWERS OF THE AGE TO COME are the seven thunders. In Revelation 10, John received a scroll and announced the voices of the seven thunders. However, he was told to seal up what the seven thunders had spoken and to not write it down. This reveals to us the seven thunders were a voice of mysteries on hold until the age to come.

The voice of the seven thunders are the voice of the powers of the age to come. This voice is the voice of Christ the King of Redemption residing in the internal of His ready vessels. And this voice of Christ the King, the voice of the seven thunders, reveals the mysteries of the powers of the age to come in the internal of HIS ready vessels.

AS THE CHOSEN VESSELS GOVERN THIS NATION AND THE EARTH, ALL GOVERNING COMES FORTH FROM THE INTERNAL WHERE THE POWERS OF THE AGE TO COME COMPRISED OF THE SEVEN SPIRITS OF GOD AND THE SEVEN THUNDERS

RESIDE. THE MIND OF CHRIST RESIDES IN THE INTERNAL AND ALL GOVERNING IS IDENTIFIED IN THE INTERNAL AND COMES FORTH FROM THE INTERNAL THROUGH THE VOICES, THE SPOKEN WORDS OF THE CHOSEN.

These mysteries of the vastness of Christ which include a love which will do more than we ever thought His power would do, as well as new judgments coming upon the Earth for the unrepentant wicked, are expressed through the Sevenfold Spirits of God. From the Sevenfold Sprits, the powers of the age to come are released. **Each of the Sevenfold Sprits when expressed from the internal of a ready vessel produces the powers of the age to come.**

The powers of the age to come were put into the future of the age to come in the same way the seven thunders were put in the future, and John was directed to not write them down. But now they come together! One and the same!

The mysteries of the seven thunders come forth, expressing the powers of the age to come, which are the expressions of the Sevenfold Spirits of God!

- **BECAUSE THEY ARE ALL HIM!**
- **THEY ARE ALL CHRIST THE KING OF REDEMPTION!**
- **THE SEVENFOLD SPIRITS ARE HIM!**
- **THE SEVEN THUNDERS ARE HIM!**

AND ULTIMATELY, THE POWERS OF THE AGE TO COME ARE EXPRESSIONS OF HIM NOW COMING FORTH!

RESIDING IN THE INTERNAL OF HIS READY VESSELS, AND COMING FORTH INTO THE EXTERNAL TO CHANGE THINGS, REARRANGE THINGS, AND TO CARRY FORTH THE DAY OF VENGEANCE OF OUR GOD!

THE POWERS OF THE AGE TO COME are the Sevenfold Spirits of God.

- They are the divine order OF HEAVEN!
- They are the eyes which are flames of fire.
- They are His sword sharp tongue.

The powers of the age to come are the TRUTH we are to buy and not sell (Proverbs 23:23), for there is to be no compromise, and the powers of the age to come do not contain even a moat of compromise.

AS I WAS WRITING THIS CHAPTER HE SPOKE AND SAID, ***"MY CHOSEN ARE TO BE AS PURE GOLD."*** Revelation 3:18... ***"I council you to buy from me, gold refined in the fire so you can become rich, and white clothes to wear, so you can cover your shameful nakedness, and salve to put on your eyes, so you can see."*** He was speaking to the church of Laodecia, who had become complacent. He was stating He wished they were hot or cold, but because of being lukewarm, He would vomit them out. But then He directs them to buy gold. And tells them the one who conquers will be granted to sit with HIM on His throne. Buying gold refined in HIS FIRE is the remedy or the solution to the complacency. The gold granted them a seat on His throne!

- THOSE WHO SIT ON HIS THRONE ARE HIS OVERCOMERS!
- THEY ARE HIS READY VESSELS!
- THEY ARE THE MANCHILD!
- THEY ARE THOSE THIS BOOK AND *'THE BLIND DATE'* WERE WRITTEN FOR. THEY ARE HIS GOLD!

When a person is truly saved, which far supersedes any form of religious or emotional experience, but when a person is truly saved, they receive a seed of salvation. We know the seed can fall on the way side, in the rocks, or even be sown into shallow ground, which all devours the seed of salvation if not watered well.

Within the internal of those who are truly saved, and who remain saved, the seed of our great salvation grows into HIS LIFE and increases in maturity of HIS LIFE. These vessels truly of Him, when they were planted in their mother's womb, received a seed of HIS DNA planted in their internal. **This is the Overcomers DNA. IT IS NOT THE SAME SEED AS THE SEED OF SALVATION. THE SEED OF HIS DNA GROWS INTO AN INTERNAL POSSESSION OF THE GOVERNMENT OF HEAVEN.** As the person/vessel became truly saved, and grew in their salvation, allowing it to grow into the LIFE of Christ, and not fall by the wayside, or among the rocks, or be sewn into shallow ground, but rather grow in the Life of Christ, they ALSO had the growing of the seed of His DNA which is the seed of the POWERS OF THE AGE TO COME.

THE VERY DRIVE AND THE VERY ABILITY TO OVERCOME EVERY TIME THEY FELL DOWN OR FELL BACK IS THE SEED OF THE POWERS OF THE AGE TO COME!

- IT IS THE SEED OF HIS DNA!
- IT HAS BEEN THERE ALL ALONG!
- AND HAS COME TO FULL MATURITY!
- IT CANNOT BE MOCKED!
- ALL ATTEMPTED MOCKERY WILL IMMEDIATELY FALL TO THE GROUND. EXPOSED!

This does not mean darkness will not at least attempt to come against what HE is doing. It means it will fail. In the age to come of the powers of the age to come, darkness will be weaker when confronting HIS LIGHT than ever before.

THE POWERS OF THE AGE TO COME are not what we might call unheard of, yet to be revealed, off the chart, signs, wonders, and miracles. There will indeed be never before seen signs, wonders and miracles. However, these events are the byproduct, or the fruit, of THE POWERS OF THE AGE TO COME, though they are not the powers in and of themselves. They are the proof of the powers!

THE POWERS ARE HIM! THE POWERS ARE HIS SEVENFOLD SPIRITS AND HIS SEVEN THUNDERS!

THE POWERS OF THE AGE TO COME ARE PRODUCED FROM THE INTERNAL OF HIS CHOSEN VESSELS. AS THE LIGHT OF CHRIST THE KING COMES FORTH IN THE INTERNAL, IT IS THE LIGHT OF THE SEVENFOLD SPIRITS OF GOD. As this light in the internal is governed by the vessel into the external, we will see, encounter, and experience the evidence of internal governmental authority. ***"They overcame him by the blood of the lamb and the word of their testimony",*** is the testimony, the evidence, the external proof, of the internal LIFE of Christ, which is the light of the Sevenfold Spirits of God, which are the powers of the age to come!

The testimony is the evidence! They overcame him/satan, by the blood of the Lamb, and by the evidence, the external proof of the internal Life, which is the light of the Sevenfold Spirits of God. The powers of the age to come!

- ➲ THIS PRODUCES THE EXACT REPRESENTATION OF CHRIST IN THE EARTH!

- ➲ THE POWERS OF THE AGE TO COME BRING RESTORATION TO ALL THINGS FROM THE GARDEN OF EDEN AND ONWARD.

The internal of His chosen vessels becomes the courtroom of Heaven from which all governing takes place. It takes place in the internal knowings which is the internal Life of

Christ, the Mind of Christ, and comes forth through the Ruah LIFE BREATH of God with the spoken word.

The internal knowings of Christ are also our thoughts! I am speaking of redeemed thoughts. Not the thoughts of the fallen mind! But when a vessel has matured in the internal LIFE and LIGHT of Christ, in the Sevenfold Spirits of God, the powers of the age to come, the knowings of the Mind of Christ take over their personal thoughts and they are the thoughts/knowings of the Mind of Christ. At this point of maturity the equipped vessel can speak the words of governing. **THEY CAN EVEN THINK THE WORDS OF GOVERNING WITHOUT THE VOCAL SPEAKING! Because their thoughts are expressions of HIS MIND!**

There will be no arguments or debates as to who the true vessels of Christ the King of Redemption are. There will be no confusion. This does not mean everyone on Earth, or our nation will accept them, embrace them, come to agreement with them, and be part of them. It just means there will be no confusion as to who they are. IT WILL BE OBVIOUS! **Not only will these vessels be obvious, there will be those who will try and imitate or mock this internal possession, which produces external manifestations of the powers of the age to come. Oh, but what a mistake! This cannot be mocked or imitated! All wolves in sheep's clothing will be exposed! Throughout time there has been so much deception and hypocrisy, but there will be no way to fake what HE is doing in the internal and bringing forth into the external from the vessels possessing the powers of the age to come.**

And even though the vessels possessed with the antichrist spirit will perform lying signs and wonders, these signs and wonders are lying because they do not come within the bookends of governmental authority. **Discernment of all lying signs and wonders lies within the book ends of government authority. The point meaning, if there is no existence of**

the governmental authority of Heaven operated by the Sevenfold Spirits of God, the powers of the age to come, prior to and following these signs and wonders, they are lying signs and wonders. The absence of true governmental authority of Heaven identifies the deception of the lying signs and wonders.

ALL SIGNS AND WONDERS OF THE POWERS OF THE AGE TO COME, THE FRUITS OF THE SEVENFOLD SPIRITS OF GOD, WILL BE SURROUNDED BY THE GOVERNMENTAL AUTHORITY OF HEAVEN!

Although satan comes as an angel of light to masquerade, which means he is a literal mask of deception, even his masquerade of false light which has deceived and been a masquerade of deception all along will no longer prevail against the internal light of the powers of the age to come. This is when ***"depart from me, I never knew you",*** truly plays out. This is when those who have operated from gifts, but not from the seed of His internal Life will be made evident! This is when "shout it from the rooftops" becomes a reality. Nothing will be hidden. Everything will be exposed.

When Christ the King of Redemption removes these vessels from the Earth to bring them to Him and fully possess them and send them back, as they leave to go to Christ the King for the full equipping, the Holy Spirit will leave with them.

True believers still on Earth, not chosen to be this first corporate group of manifested sons, who have the Holy Spirit within their being will not lose the Holy Spirit. He will remain with them! However, the Holy Spirit will leave the Earth.

He is the restrainer. He has restrained all evil not yet allowed by Holy God until the time of His removal. When He is removed, the restraining is removed, and prior restrained evil and darkness will be allowed. This extreme darkness will attempt to confront the extreme light in His chosen vessels, but it will not prevail! There will be no comparison!

The light of the powers of the age to come will expose and outshine all evil and all darkness.

Hence producing the most foolish time of mankind to try and mock what God is doing!

THE POWERS OF THE AGE TO COME ARE THE PERFECT DESCRIPTION OF WHAT LIFE WILL BE LIKE, 'WHEN HE COMES'!

EVEN SO LORD, COME!

NOTES

Chapter 8
STRENGTHEN THAT WHICH REMAINS!

Everything He is saying and doing from here on out is absolutely defying logic.

Revelation 3:2 instructs us to strengthen that which remains.

Revelation 3:2, ***"The One having THE SEVEN SPIRITS OF GOD,*** (CHRIST THE KING), SPEAKS AND SAYS, ***you must be WATCHING and STRENGTHEN THAT WHICH REMAINS, that which is on the point of rejection, because I have not found your works completed before my God."***

Because the Kingdom of God is within, not external, but now internal, we must strengthen that which remains, which is the seed of our salvation, combined with the seed of the DNA of Christ, with the outcome of HIS LIFE coming forth in maturity much greater than the seed.

'WHEN HE COMES', He is coming to those whom the Kingdom of God WITHIN has been strengthened, and which greatly remains with evidence of HIS LIFE, THE SEVENFOLD SPIRITS OF GOD, THE POWERS OF THE AGE TO COME, residing within. Residing in the internal of the vessel for THE KINGDOM OF GOD IS WITHIN!

If you have read *'THE BLIND DATE, THE MISSING LINK TO BRIDAL READINESS'*, along with or prior to this book, *'WHEN HE COMES'*, you have read and processed a lot. It might even seem overwhelming. But plain and simple above all we must know this is a sovereign move. He has sovereignly chosen His vessels.

IT IS IMPERATIVE WE NOT OVERLOOK, NOR FORGET THAT EVERYTHING HE IS SAYING AND DOING WITHIN HIS SOVEREIGN MOVE DEFIES LOGIC. IT GOES DIRECTLY AGAINST THE ANALYTICAL MIND OF MAN. IT IS OFFENSIVE TO THE MIND OF MAN.

IN ORDER TO EMBRACE AS WELL AS MOVE FORWARD IN WHAT HE IS CURRENTLY DOING, WE MUST OVERCOME

EVERY OFFENSE AND WALK INTO THE BREAKTHROUGH HE IS BRINGING.

- 💣 You are either a sovereignly chosen vessel who understands every bit of this,

- 💣 Or, a sovereignly chosen vessel just now catching on to what He is indeed doing,

- 💣 Or one to receive the Kingdom of God within from these sovereignly chosen vessels when they return from His Bosom.

Either way, the truth within these books was written for you! IT IS NOT HIS WILL ANY OF THOSE TRULY HIS BE LEFT OUT!

The compressed version of these books is as follows, but do not only read this portion. Read the entirety of both books so you are fully ready for your role in the Kingdom of Christ the King about to enter the Earth in HIS SECOND COMING.

'THE BLIND DATE' is when we get to know Christ the King. A King we have never known. The King who was part of the Trinity even in the foundations of the Earth. Jesus of Nazareth was never supposed to be needed, but when Adam and Eve introduced the fall of mankind, God Almighty sent us a savior, Jesus of Nazareth. Christ the King is the King we have never known! He is the King who has waited since the foundations of the Earth in the beginning of time for His turn. HE HAS WAITED FOR US TO ENTER INTO THE VASTNESS OF WHO HE TRULY IS, for His rule and His reign on the Earth in the internal of His vessels. This is why HE must come forth on a BLIND DATE and we must get to know HIM! THE BLIND DATE OF THE VASTNESS OF CHRIST THE KING WHOM WE HAVE NEVER KNOWN ABSOLUTELY DEFIES ALL LOGIC.

The 'MISSING LINK' is letting go of Jesus of Nazareth. Allowing Christ the King to annihilate Jesus of Nazareth because His job was finished on the cross. Allowing Christ the King to annihilate Jesus of Nazareth, so God's original intention of Christ the King on hold since the foundation of the Earth can come forth in the fullness of His glory and power. The powers of the age to come! We are not dogging out Jesus. It is Christ the King HIMSELF who is annihilating Jesus of Nazareth because His time was up a long time ago. It is now time for Christ the King! We are the ones who have continued to make everything about Jesus of Nazareth. But Christ the King is saying IT IS MY TIME NOW!

THE ANNIHILATION OF JESUS OF NAZARETH DEFIES LOGIC. IT DEFIES THE MIND OF MAN AND WHAT WE HAVE ALWAYS THOUGHT WE KNEW.

He is annihilating the paradigm of Himself and how HE's always done things. Everything He is doing is internal, therefore the possession of Christ the King is internal.

When we continue to do it the old way through external studying, research, etc., we learn a lot, but the internal possession does not take place.

The internal possession of Christ, the Kingdom of God within, takes place as He speaks internally with His Life voice. He abides in the internal kingdom, and as His vessels we govern from the internal kingdom.

There is a vast difference between those learning the truth of what He's currently doing by way of research and those learning what He's currently doing by way of the INTERNAL LIFE BREATH! It's happening within those learning by the way of internal Life. It's happening in those who have been willing to walk away from the old ways of Jesus of Nazareth and allow

HIM to annihilate the paradigm of HIMSELF! Our role is to respond to HIS annihilation.

Those who have strengthened the seed of salvation and the seed of His DNA, those who have strengthened the Sevenfold Spirits of God, and the Powers of The Age to Come within are those in whom Christ the King is about to manifest HIS SECOND COMING!

At this point, your role is,

- to either catch up and become one,
- continue to mature as one,
- or honor and anticipate those who are coming, for the Kingdom of God will be within them.

They are the vessels of THE SECOND COMING OF CHRIST and everyone who has not become one of them will search them out, run to them, join up with them, receive from them, and be protected by them.

AS HE CHANGES THINGS, REARRANGES THINGS, AND DISPLAYS THE DAY OF VENGEANCE OF A HOLY GOD TO SET THINGS STRAIGHT AND MAKE THINGS RIGHT............ EVERYTHING HE IS SAYING AND DOING FROM HERE ON OUT IS ABSOLUTELY DEFYING LOGIC!

ON EARTH, AS IT IS IN HEAVEN!

YES, YES, YES, AND AMEN!

NOTES

IT IS ALL Sovereign!

It is HIS move, but it is also His sovereign time. When God is in a sovereign move, we cannot stop it. He moves forward within His sovereign move. In the same way we cannot stop a sovereign move, we also cannot initiate a sovereign move.

In 2017 HE spoke and said, "It is time for THE SOVEREIGN things of God to overtake the natural!"

He began His sovereign move in 2022. He is overtaking the natural and fallen mind of man with HIS SOVEREIGN MOVE OF REDEMPTION TO HIS ORIGINAL INTENTION.

Don't make the choice to miss out. No one before us has had this opportunity because it is sovereign. Four years ago He said, "***He was 'about' to make the move NO ONE was YET aware of***." **He is NOW making His sovereign move and we are VERY aware. IT IS happening, and it's about to FULLY burst forth.**

It's all sovereign! Meaning never before has anyone who has walked the face of this Earth had this opportunity since the fall of mankind in the garden.

Never has God initiated the sovereign move of redemption unto the original intention until NOW. But WE have this opportunity. We have this gift. We have this chance.

- Don't be a bystander.
- Don't be an on looker.
- Be a full participant!

THE KING IS ACTIVELY COMING!

NOTES

www.ingramcontent.com/pod-product-compliance
Lightning Source LLC
LaVergne TN
LVHW010933110826
845149LV00013B/2570

* 9 7 9 8 9 9 4 3 8 7 3 2 0 *